# CONSTITUTIONALISM – HUMAN RIGHTS – SEPARATION OF POWERS

# Constitutional Law Library

1. F. Laursen (Ed.), *The Treaty of Nice: Actor Preferences, Bargaining and Institutional Choice* (2006)

2. T. Barkhuysen and S.D. Lindenbergh (Eds), *Constitutionalisation of Private Law* (2006)

3. J. Nergelius (Ed.), *Nordic and Other European Constitutional Traditions* (2006)

4. G.M. Pikis, *Constitutionalism – Human Rights – Separation of Powers: The Cyprus Precedent* (2006)

# Constitutionalism – Human Rights – Separation of Powers

## The Cyprus Precedent

By

*Georghios M. Pikis*

*Judge of the International Criminal Court*
*Formerly President of the Supreme Court of Cyprus*

MARTINUS NIJHOFF PUBLISHERS
LEIDEN / BOSTON

A C.I.P. record for this book is available from the Library of Congress.

*Printed on acid-free paper.*

ISSN: 1871-4110
ISBN-13: 978-90-04-15241-0
ISBN-10: 90-04-15241-5


Koninklijke Brill NV incorporates the imprints Brill Academic Publishers, Martinus Nijhoff Publishers and VSP.

http://www.brill.nl



Printed and bound in The Netherlands.

**To my beloved son Antonis**

# Contents

# Acknowledgment

I wish to acknowledge the help given me by Franziska Eckelmans, my legal assistant, for the transcription of the text, meticulous proof reading and her astute observations about the structure of the book. Moreover, her perceptive mind was a constant aid in avoiding pitfalls. For the help given me I express my great appreciation.

# List of Abbreviations

| | |
|---|---|
| a.o. | and others/and another |
| All E.R. | All England Law Reports |
| C.L.R. | Cyprus Law Reports |
| D.L.R. | Dominion Law Reports |
| E.H.R.R. | European Human Rights Reports |
| J. | Justice of the Supreme Court |
| L | Law |
| L.Ed. | Lawyers' Edition, United States Supreme Court Reports |
| No. | Number |
| Nos. | Numbers |
| p. | Page |
| P. | President of the Supreme Court |
| P.C. | Privacy Council |
| P.L.R. | Pakistan Law Reports |
| R.S.C.C. | Reports of the Supreme Constitutional Court |
| v. | versus |
| W.P. | Pakistan Law Reports, West Pakistan Series |
| (CA) | Court of Appeal (a bench normally composed of three Judges of the Supreme Court) |
| (FB) | Full Bench of the Supreme Court |
| (P) | Plenum of the Supreme Court |
| (SJ) | Single Judge of the Supreme Court |

# Table of cases of the Supreme Court of Cyprus

Reference is made to chapter and paragraph number

# A

## Preface

Cyprus became an independent State in 1960. It was endowed with a Constitution evolved within the parameters of the Zurich Agreement concluded between the Greek and Turkish Prime Ministers in February 1959 and the London Conference that followed later the same month. This conference was attended, in addition to Greece and Turkey, by the leadership of the Greek and Turkish Cypriots and the colonial power, the Government of the United Kingdom. The agreements leading to the drafting and subsequent establishment of the Constitution of Cyprus came to be known as the London-Zurich Agreements. It took the parties nearly a year and a half to finalize the Constitution that came into force on the day of Cyprus' independence. *1*

The law applicable at the time of the formal proclamation of Cyprus as an independent state on 16th August 1960 was, with few exceptions, English law, as codified in a number of statutes that served as the prototype for its introduction in British colonies. The Constitution of Cyprus retained the law applicable prior to independence subject to such modifications as necessary to bring it into conformity with the Constitution. Subject to this proviso continuity of law was assured in the nascent state. The adjustments necessary to bring pre-existing law into accord with the Constitution were neither insignificant nor peripheral. *2*

The Constitution introduced a new legal order having no direct affinity to English law. Whereas under English law Parliament is supreme and *3* omnipotence is acknowledged to the Legislature "Queen in Parliament",[1] under the new legal order in Cyprus the Constitution is proclaimed to be the supreme law. Authority for action in every sphere of government must derive from the Constitution and must be exercised in accordance with the norms stipulated therein.

*4* Given the supremacy of the Constitution, extensive mechanism is provided for testing the constitutionality of laws, rules and regulations as well as decisions, acts or omissions emanating from the exercise of executive or administrative authority.

*5* Unlike the United Kingdom, the three powers of the State are institutionally separated and the domain of each is charted in the Constitution. As often acknowledged in judicial decisions, the principle or doctrine of separation of powers permeates every aspect of the Constitution; transgression of the boundaries of its authority by anyone of the three powers renders its action unconstitutional and on that account invalid.

*6* Judicial review of administrative action introduced by the Constitution is institutionalized along the lines that kindred jurisdiction finds expression in continental law. Judicial review as a separate jurisdiction for the examination of the legality of acts, decisions and omissions of the Administration was first established in France in the Napoleonic era "1799", assigned to the Conseil d'État, a separate branch of the Judiciary. Judicial review of administrative action was meant to serve as a bulwark against arbitrary rule. Prior to independence judicial review of administrative action as an autonomous branch of judicial power was unknown to the British colony of Cyprus. Such limited scope for the review of administrative action that existed derived from the jurisdiction to issue prerogative writs, namely certiorari, prohibition, mandamus, and quo warranto.[2] The Constitution expressly retained jurisdiction to issue the aforementioned writs as part of the

[1] The sovereignty of Parliament was in substance if not in form mitigated to an extent by the accession of the UK to the European Communities in 1973 and the incorporation into domestic law of the human rights guaranteed by the European Convention on Human Rights and Protocols by the enactment of the Human Rights Act 1998 that came into force in the year 2000.

[2] Gradually, judicial review of administrative action gained ground in England. The milestones in that direction were a) The decision in Anisminic v. Foreign Compensation etc. (1969) 1 All E.R. 208; b) The institutional and statutory reforms of 1977 and 1981; and c) The establishment of an administrative court as a branch of the High Court of Justice in the year 2000 (See Practice Note (2000) 4 All E.R. 1071).

armoury of the judicial power (see Article 155.4) confining their application (see *Ramadan v. Republic 1 R.S.C.C. 49*[3]) to areas lying outside the domain of the revisional jurisdiction of the Supreme Constitutional Court established under Article 146. Habeas corpus jurisdiction entitling the High Court to test the legality of deprivation of liberty deriving from English law was retained by Article 155.4.

Judicial review as fashioned under Article 146 is modelled on the continental precedent, finding application not only in France but in many other countries of continental Europe too. The process of judicial review entails inquiry into the legality of executive and administrative action or inaction introducing thereby the inquisitorial system of justice in that sphere of jurisdiction parallel to the adversarial system of justice that finds application in civil and criminal proceedings.

The entrenchment of fundamental rights and liberties of the individual, *7*
customarily referred to as the human rights of a person, is a salient feature of the Constitution.

Chapter II of the Constitution (Articles 6 to 35 inclusive) guarantees human rights as a basic aspect of constitutional order accompanied by comprehensive mechanism for their protection. The interpretation, identification of their purport and range of application of human rights have been the subject of a vast body of case law. Most decisions on the constitutionality of laws, regulations, acts and decisions of the Administration revolve around their compatibility with human rights and the doctrine of separation of powers.

The background to the establishment of the State of Cyprus, the bitter com- *8*
promises made in relation to the rights of members of the two communities reflected in the Constitution, generated mistrust between the Greeks and the Turks of Cyprus that erupted into intercommunal strife at the end of 1963 spilling over into the year following. To sustain constitutional order and ensure the viability of the State, recourse was had to the law or doctrine of necessity. Regrettably, the circumstances that led to the invocation of the law of necessity did not eclipse; on the contrary, they were exacerbated by the coup d'état staged on 15 July 1974 by the military Junta that ruled Greece (a guarantor power of Cyprus' independence) at the time, aimed at toppling the democratically elected government; a blow to the country, followed five days later by a bigger and far more catastrophic one, the Turkish (another guarantor power of Cyprus' independence) invasion of Cyprus.

[3] The judgment of the Court was read by Forsthoff P.

The invasion and sequential occupation by Turkey of a large part of the island, entailing the partition of the country in two, was accompanied by the displacement of the majority of the inhabitants (Greek Cypriots) from the occupied area with the obvious aim of establishing two ethnically homogenous regions; an objective that was soon after brought about. Notwithstanding the calamities that befell Cyprus, the rule of law never abated and none of the fundamental rights and liberties of the individual were limited, restricted or suspended. The Constitution continued to provide the basis for the rule of the country. Judicial decisions relevant to the law of necessity illuminate the principles surrounding its application. These principles are explained in numerous decisions. The raison d'être of the law of necessity as expounded in Cyprus case law met with the approval of the Supreme Court of Canada in the case of *Language Rights under the Manitoba Act 1870 (1985) 19 D.L.R. (4th) 1.*

*9* The independence of the Judiciary is institutionally and functionally guaranteed by the Cyprus Constitution. The appointment, promotion, transfer, termination of appointment, dismissal and the exercise of disciplinary jurisdiction over the first instance Judiciary vest, consistently with the doctrine of separation of powers, in the High Court[4] (Article 157.2). Likewise, the retirement on grounds of mental or physical incapacity or infirmity of Superior Judges lies with the judicial authorities as does the dismissal of Judges for misconduct. In both, the case of subordinate courts and higher judiciary, the compulsory retirement on the aforementioned grounds and dismissal for misconduct can only be ordered in proceedings of a judicial nature (see Articles 153.8(3) and 154.3). The power to appoint Judges of the Supreme Court vests in the President and Vice-President of the Republic.[5] Nonetheless, in virtue of a longstanding constitutional tradition, evolved in the interests of the separateness and independence of the Judiciary, the President of the Republic invariably seeks the recommendations of the Supreme Court as to who should be appointed, which are as a rule followed. This constitutional practice is a guarantee against the politicisation of the Judiciary. The appointment of Judges of subordinate courts is made from among the ranks of successful law practitioners of certain years standing. Appointments to the Supreme Court are customarily made from among members of the first instance courts of general criminal and civil

[4] Later merged in the Supreme Court by virtue of law L-33/64.

[5] Exercised by the President after the events of 1963–1964 in virtue of the law of necessity.

jurisdiction, the District Courts. The appraisal of the Cyprus Judiciary by the EU authorities made in the context of accession negotiations is the following: "The Judiciary is independent and the separation of powers between executive, judicial and legislative branches respected. The standard of justice is high."

*10* The rule of binding precedent, a notable aspect of English law, finds application in Cyprus as in many other common law countries. Binding is the principle emerging from the application of the law to the resolution of the issue in dispute.[6] The principle distilled therefrom, referred to as the ratio decidendi of a case, deriving from judgments of the Supreme Court in the exercise of its appellate jurisdiction or its original jurisdiction exercised by the plenum of the Court is binding on hierarchically subordinate courts. The ratio of a decision of the Supreme Court given in the exercise of its jurisdiction as a final court is, subject to well-recognized exceptions, binding on the Supreme Court itself. Amenity to depart from earlier decisions is acknowledged whenever the Court concludes that a previous decision is founded on a) an incontrovertibly wrong principle, b) a principle of law leading with manifest injustice and c) a principle irreconcilable to changed circumstances.[7] Thus, where the raison d'être of the ratio of a case is correlated to the circumstances prevailing at the time of its delivery, departure from precedent can be justified by reference to the disappearance of the foundation upon which the legal principle rests.

*11* I practised at the Bar of Cyprus for five years between 1961 and 1966 and served for many years as a Judge; thereafter a trial Judge (District Judge, President District Court) from 1966 to 1981, Justice of the Supreme Court of Cyprus from 1981 to 1995 and President of the Supreme Court from 1995 to 2004, when I resigned my position to take up full time duties as a Judge of the International Criminal Court. The object of this book is to trace the development of constitutional law in Cyprus as reflected in the case law of the Supreme Court and its forerunners, the Supreme Constitutional Court and the High Court of Cyprus. Judgment writing in

---

[6] Eleftheriou-Kanga v. Republic (1989) 3 C.L.R. 262.

[7] Republic v. D. Demetriades (1977) 3 C.L.R. 213; Republic v. Thalassinou (1991) 3 C.L.R. 203; Nicolaou a.o. v. Nicolaou a.o. (No. 2) (1992) 1 C.L.R. 1328; Republic v. Yiallourou (1995) 3 C.L.R. 363; Mavrogenis v. House of Representatives a.o. (No. 3) (1996) 1 C.L.R. 315; in relation to the evolution of the principle of binding precedent in England – see inter alia Practice Statement of the House of Lords – Note (1966) 3 All E.R. 77, R. v. Shivpuri (1986) 2 All E.R. 334, 345 (HL).

the Supreme Court and in subordinate courts follows English tradition. The material facts defining the dispute are recounted and resolved whenever in conflict by clear findings of fact against the background of the law bearing on the issues in dispute. The Supreme Court presently consisting of the President and 12 Justices sits in benches of three, five, seven or en banc in exercise of its appellate jurisdiction and sits singly in exercise of its original jurisdiction[8] other than its constitutional or electoral jurisdiction. The judgments of the Court in the exercise of its original jurisdiction issued by the single Judge are subject to appeal before a bench composed of no less than five Judges of the Supreme Court. In the exercise of its original constitutional jurisdiction and its original jurisdiction as an electoral court, the Supreme Court sits in plenum.

Judgments of appellate benches and the plenum reflecting a unanimous, a majority or a minority decision are eponymously delivered. In case of unanimity, one or more decisions may be given under the name of the Judge or Judges who assume responsibility for their preparation. A judgment given on behalf of more than one Judges reflects the opinion of the totality of them. Not infrequently more than one judgments are given concurring in the result. Of course, dissenting Judges write their own judgment or judgments, as the case may be, under their name. In the above sense, I was the author of many judgments of the Supreme Court reflecting majority opinions, concurring opinions and not infrequently dissent. The names of the Judges, who delivered decisions cited in this book, will be recorded in footnotes. Reference will not be made to all cases but to a number of them giving expression to a principle of law, identifying or exemplifying the sphere of its application. The exercise is confined to a review of the case law that emerged by the time of my departure from the Supreme Court in March 2004.

In distilling the principles of the law deriving from decided cases, care was taken to represent them with such clarity as I could master and as precisely as possible .

[8] Revisional jurisdiction under Article 146 and Admiralty jurisdiction conferred upon the Supreme Court by the Courts of Justice Law (L-14/60).

# B

# Constitutional Framework

## I. Survey of the Constitution

The Constitution of Cyprus is divided into 13 Parts and 199 Articles. It is a detailed document that makes provision for virtually every aspect of the Administration of the country and prescribes the rules governing the exercise of the powers entrusted to organs of government. Part I, headed "General Provisions", identifies the premises upon which the Republic of Cyprus is founded. Part II, entitled "Fundamental rights and liberties", stipulates for and guarantees the rights of the individual. Given the scope and breadth of the entrenched rights, discernible from their content and sphere of application, it can justly be said that Part II of the Constitution provides an extensive charter of human rights though not an exhaustive one. A drawback of this chapter is that the application of certain human rights is qualified by reference to the community to which persons belong, Greek or Turkish. A percentage of 30 percent of positions in the Executive, the Legislature, the public service and the security forces (police and gendarmerie) and a percentage of 40 percent of posts in the army is assured to members of the Turkish community making up only 18 percent of the population as opposed to the Greek community making up 82 percent of the population to which the remaining percentage of posts and offices is allotted. Thus, merit ceases to be the sole qualification for appointment to the 1 public service. The acknowledgment of human rights to persons by reference to factors extraneous to human identity is an antinomy to the very concept and object of human rights.

2 The competence, authority and jurisdiction of the three powers of the State are defined in different Parts of the Constitution (executive power – Part III, legislative power – Part IV, judicial power – Parts IX and X). Each of the three branches of government is referred to in terms as a power, a fact indicative in itself of the status of each pillar of the State (see Articles 54, 61 and 152). At no stage does the authority of one power of the State converge upon that of another; nor is there any element of subordination of one power to another.

Save for communal matters, state power is allocated in its entirety to the legislative, executive and judicial branches of government trusted to function coordinately for the promotion of individual and common good. Each power of the State is autonomous in its domain, self-sustaining and functionally independent. Subject to the Constitution, power is conferred upon each branch of the State to regulate its proceedings. Educational, cultural and matters pertaining to cooperative societies of the Greek and Turkish communities are assigned respectively to Greek and Turkish Communal Chambers (Part V of the Constitution).

## II. The Supremacy of the Constitution

3 The Constitution is declared to be the supreme law of the land – Article 179.1. Article 179.1 reads:

> This Constitution shall be the supreme law of the Republic.

Article 179 establishes on the one hand the supremacy of the Constitution and on the other prohibits the enactment of any law, rule or regulation or the issuing of any act or decision by any organ or authority of the State that is contrary to or inconsistent with the Constitution. This prohibition is prescribed in absolute terms in Article 179.2. It reads:

> No law or decision of the House of Representatives or of any of the Communal Chambers and no act or decision of any organ, authority or person in the Republic exercising executive power or any administrative function shall in any way be repugnant to, or inconsistent with, any of the provisions of this Constitution.

Compatibility with the Constitution is a *sine qua non* for the validity of any act of State authority. This is the cardinal and all pervasive norm of the Constitution; the bedrock of constitutional order.

The principle embodied in Article 179 is underpinned by a series of provisions of the Constitution establishing the necessary means for testing the constitutionality of laws, by-laws, acts, decisions as well as omissions of the legislative and executive powers.

## III. Constitutional Review

Article 140 provides mechanism for the pre-emptive control of the constitutionality of laws or decisions of the Legislature. The President and Vice-President of the Republic[9] are empowered to refer the constitutionality of any law or decision of the House of Representatives or any part thereof before their promulgation in the official gazette to the Supreme Constitutional Court for its opinion. Such reference must be made within the time limited for publication, that is within 15 days from the day the law or decision in question is transmitted by the House of Representatives to the President of the Republic for promulgation. In proceedings under Article 140, the President of the Republic and the House of Representatives are heard on the constitutional issue raised for consideration. If the law or decision is found to be unconstitutional it lapses. It does not reach the statute book. Likewise, if a distinct part of the law or decision is found to be unconstitutional provided it can be severed from the remaining parts of the law or decision in question, as the case may be, it is promulgated stripped of its offensive provisions. *4*

Under Articles 137, 138, 141, 142 and 143 power is conferred upon the President and Vice-President of the Republic to refer the constitutionality of specific laws[10] to the Supreme Court by way of reference or through a recourse *5*

[9] The President after the necessitous circumstances of 1963–1964.

[10] Category of laws: a) laws discriminating against either community; b) discriminatory provisions of the budget; c) laws prescribing conditions, formalities or restrictions in the exercise of the rights safeguarded by Article 25 ensuring freedom to practise any profession, to carry on any occupation, trade or business with a view to determining whether they are in the public interest; d) laws or decisions of the Communal Chambers on grounds of repugnancy to or inconsistency with the Constitution; e) legislation by an outgoing House of Representatives entitled – in the presence of exceptional circumstances – to legislate a precondition under Article 68 pending the assumption of duties by the newly elected House of Representatives.

for the determination of their constitutionality. Articles 138, 141, 142 and 143 make provision for a pre-emptive species of control of the constitutionality of laws, whereas Article 137 envisages a recourse, the filing of which shall suspend the operation of the impugned law pending the decision of the Court.

6 Article 144 makes provision for what may be termed remedial or sequential review of the constitutionality of laws or decisions or any part thereof within the context of judicial proceedings. Neither the Constitution nor any law or the Rules of Court legitimise *actio popularis*, that is the initiation of judicial proceedings in the name of the law by a disinterested party (*Pitsillos v. C.B.C. (1982) 3 C.L.R. 208* (*FB*)[11]). A review of the constitutionality of a law or decision of the House of Representatives will be undertaken if adjudication upon the issue is material for the determination of the dispute in pending judicial proceedings or a distinct part thereof. It is for the court seized of the judicial cause to decide whether adjudication upon the constitutional issue raised is material for the outcome of the proceedings; if not the issue will not be addressed. As much has been affirmed in many judicial decisions. Indicative of the approach of the Supreme Court to the subject is a fairly recent case – *Alfa Concrete Ltd. a.o. v. Thoma (2001) 1 C.L.R. 594*[12] *(CA)* – where it was repeated that the Court will not probe an issue of constitutionality unless the exercise is necessary for the determination of the case before the court. The Court expressed serious reservations whether it is at all possible to address an issue of constitutionality of a law preliminary to the hearing of a criminal case.

7 Article 139 provides for the resolution of conflicts and contests of power or competence between organs or authorities of the Republic by way of recourse to the Supreme Constitutional Court vested with jurisdiction to void any law or decision issued without power or competence and to remedy the ill effects of constitutional disorder by annulling the law, act or decision issued without constitutional authorization.

8 Contrariety to the Constitution is a distinct ground for annulling a decision, act or omission of the Administration in the context of judicial review of administrative or executive action under Article 146.1.

[11] Judgment delivered by Pikis J.
[12] Judgment delivered by Pikis P.

## IV. Bringing Pre-Independence Legislation into Conformity with the Constitution

As explained in the Preface, legislation in force at the time of independence was saved subject to such modifications necessary to bring it into accord with the Constitution. Article 188.1 provides that pre-existing laws, rules and regulations shall be construed and applied with such modifications as may be necessary to bring them into conformity with the Constitution. To the term "modification" a broad meaning is attached by paragraph 5 of the same Article. It includes "amendment, adaptation and repeal". Power to adapt pre-existing legislation to the Constitution is vested in the Judiciary exercised in the context of pending judicial proceedings (see Article 188.4). The need to adjust pre-existing laws to the dictates of the Constitution has not been obviated by the translation of pre-independence legislation pursuant to the provisions of the Official Languages of the Constitution Law L-150/91 1989, as expressly decided in *Mohamed (1998) 1 C.L.R. 1304 (P)*,[13] nor has the text in its original form lost its authenticity in case of conflict with the translation. The scrutiny of legislation with a view to determining its compatibility with the Constitution is in the nature of things a judicial function. Consequently, the power given to the Court to pronounce on the compatibility of a law, rule or regulation with the Constitution and on that account in a proper case declare it to be extinct, lies within the parameters of the judicial power. Questions of principle arise in relation to the power conferred upon the Court to amend or adapt such legislation to the requisites of constitutional order. Adaptation and more so amendment import an element of choice respecting the content of legislation, hard to reconcile with the attributes of judicial power or the system of separation of powers. The anomaly was largely remedied by the disinclination of the Supreme Court to approve modifications or adaptations of such legislation except when the substitute is obvious, evident from the tenor and spirit of the law. *9*

Below, reference will be made to a number of decided cases illuminating the interpretation and illustrating the application of Article 188.1. In *Attorney General v. Lazarides a.o. (1992) 2 C.L.R. 8*[14] (*FB*) the Court explained that competence to harmonise pre-existing legislation with the Constitution lies *10*

---

[13] Judgment delivered by Pikis P.

[14] Majority judgment delivered by Pikis J.; a concurring judgment delivered by Poyiadjis J.

exclusively with the Judiciary; a process involving the exercise of a species of jurisdiction unrelated to any other. Unlike legislation enacted after independence, no presumption of constitutionality operates in favour of pre-existing legislation introduced outside the constitutional framework. It is the courts' duty to ensure, whenever need arises in the course of judicial proceedings that English colonial legislation conforms to the Constitution; and if not possible to declare it repealed. The drastic results that the exercise of this jurisdiction may have are exemplified by the case *Republic v. Sampson (1991) 1 C.L.R. 858 (FB)*[15], where the Supreme Court decided that the provisions of the Prison Law CAP 86[16] and Regulations made thereunder conferring power upon the Prison Authorities, a department of the Executive, to abbreviate or shorten the length of imprisonment for certain reasons was contrary to the Constitution that made the punishment of crime the sole responsibility of the judicial power of the State (Article 12.3). Any other approach would run counter to the doctrine of separation of powers. Consequently, the relevant provisions of CAP 86 and Regulations made thereunder did not survive the introduction of the Constitution. Only the President of the Republic can under the Constitution remit or commute a sentence of imprisonment (see Article 53.4). Similar was the approach of the Court to the compatibility of Section 21 of the Streets and Buildings Law CAP 96 with the Constitution in *Municipal Council of Yeroskipou a.o. v. Council of Ministers a.o. (1996) 3 C.L.R. 389 (FB)*. Section 21 empowered the Governor in Council,[17] the supreme executive and legislative body under colonial rule, to set aside decisions of a municipality for legal error. At issue was the validity of an order of the Council of Ministers setting aside a decision of the municipality of Yeroskipou for failure to comply with the provisions of the law relevant to an application for a building permit. The municipality contested by recourse under Article 139 the power of the Council of Ministers as successors to the executive authority of the Governor in Council (Article 188.3) to order the annulment of its decision. Eight[18] of the thirteen judges voided the decision of the Council of Ministers holding it

[15] Judgment delivered by Pikis J.

[16] The laws of Cyprus were codified and embodied into separate Chapters in 1959; they are referred to as CAP.

[17] The Council of Ministers after independence in relation to its executive authority (Article 188.3(b)).

[18] Judgments delivered by Artemides J. and Kallis J.

to be patently invalid, as the decision of the municipality was not legally flawed. That being the case, they did not address the issue of the possible extinction of Section 21 as a result of the order introduced by the Constitution, considering the issue immaterial for the outcome of the proceedings. The remaining five members[19] of the Court likewise concluded that the decision of the Council of Ministers was invalid but for different reasons. In their view, the question of survival of Section 21 preceded the possible application of its provisions. If the law ceased to exist on independence no question of deriving authority therefrom could arise. Section 21 was found to be in total discord with the Constitution because a) it conferred power upon a non-judicial authority to review administrative action contrary to Article 146.1, and b) it breached the doctrine of separation of powers by vesting judicial power in the Executive. They held that Section 21 ceased to be in force inasmuch as the Constitution trusted power to review the legality of administrative action exclusively to the judicial authorities of the State (Article 146.1).

The case of *Fekkas v. The Electricity Authority of Cyprus (1968) 1 C.L.R. 173 (CA)*[20] is indicative of the disinclination of the Court to engage upon a process of adaptation or amendment of pre-existing legislation, where the change to be made is not self-evident. The Electricity Development Law CAP 171 provided that claims against the Electricity Authority arising out of wrongful acts of the corporation or its employees should be raised within 3 months from the date the cause of action accrued. The Court found that the limitation period provided for by the statute was unduly restrictive, irreconcilable with the provisions of Article 30.1 guaranteeing unimpeded access to a court of law as the fundamental right of every person. Moreover, it fell foul of the provisions of Article 28 because of unequal treatment of the wronged persons compared to other individuals who were essentially in the same position but whose right of access to the Court was not restricted by such a drastic period of limitation. The Court did not proceed to substitute a period of limitation for the one declared to be unconstitutional leaving it to the Legislature to fill the gap in the law.

An instance of the Court engaging upon a process of substitution of a legal provision for the one decried as unconstitutional is provided by the

---

19 Judgment delivered by Pikis P.

20 Judgment delivered by Triantafyllides J.

case of *United Bible Societies (Gulf) v. Hadjicostas (1990) 1 C.L.R. 81 (CA)*.[21] The Civil Procedure Rules introduced during the colonial era made English, the official language at the time, the language of court proceedings. The Constitution of Cyprus made the native languages of the population, Greek and Turkish, the official languages of the country and the languages of litigation (Article 3.4).[22] In *United Bible Societies* (supra) the Court ruled that as from independence the relevant provision of the Civil Procedure Rules should read "Greek and Turkish" instead of "English". The substitution was in line with the avowed object of the Rules to make the official language of the country the language of litigation.

## V. Ambiguous Provisions of the Constitution – Interpretation

*11* Article 149(b) confers jurisdiction upon the Supreme Constitutional Court to provide an authentic interpretation of the Constitution in case of ambiguity. If one is identified, it must be resolved by reference to the letter and spirit of the Zurich and London Agreements. The jurisdiction to clarify ambiguities is of a declaratory character intended to forestall deviations from the Constitution owing to lack of clarity of its text. The jurisdiction is akin to the jurisdiction of English courts to issue declaratory judgments obviating the need to make an emerging dispute the subject of litigation. In *re Georghios Ladas a.o. (1985) 3 C.L.R. 2845*[23] (*P*)the Court was required to resolve an alleged ambiguity of the provisions of the Constitution surrounding the election of the President of the House of Representatives. The Court made it clear that Article 149(b) confers jurisdiction to resolve ambiguities of constitutional provisions affecting the functioning of the Legislature; correspondingly one may say the same about the Executive. In *Efthymiou (1991) 3 C.L.R. 299 (FB)*[24] the Court reviewed in a definitive

21 Judgment delivered by Pikis J.; see also Sofocleous a.o. v. Stylianou (1992) 1 C.L.R. 81.

22 Article 189 permitted the continuation of the use of the English language (and the text of English legislation in its original form) for an initial 5-year period that was extended by law until 1989 (see L-51/65 and L-67/88).

23 Leading judgment delivered by Triantafyllides P., minority judgment as to reasoning delivered by Pikis J.

24 Judgment delivered by Pikis J.

way the prerequisites for the assumption and exercise of jurisdiction under Article 149(b), wherefrom the following propositions may be extracted:

a) There must be a concrete dispute between two or more parties respecting the meaning of a constitutional provision, not necessarily arising in the context of judicial proceedings, before the Court assumes interpretative jurisdiction in the matter.
b) The constitutional provision in question must be prima facie ambiguous.[25] The term prima facie denotes an ambiguity evident on the face of a legal provision. It must at first blush appear to admit of more than one interpretation.
c) Article 149(b) does not provide an avenue for the declaration of the rights of the parties nor does it bestow jurisdiction to adjudicate upon the constitutionality of laws. Its ambit is confined to the resolution of a concrete dispute with regard to the meaning of an ambiguous provision of the Constitution paving the way for an informed decision by the parties.

As the authentic text of the Constitution is in two languages, Greek and Turkish, provision is made in Article 149(a) for the resolution of any conflict between the two texts of the Constitution by reference to the text of the draft of the Constitution prepared and signed in English. *12*

[25] see Menelaos Demetriou etc. (CBC Staff Society) v. Republic 1 R.S.C.C. 99; Republic v. N. P. Loftis 1 R.S.C.C. 30; Republic v. Zacharia 2 R.S.C.C. 1; Cyprus Grain Commission etc. v. New Vatyli Co-operative Society 4 R.S.C.C. 91. See re Ladas a.o. (1985) 3 C.L.R. 2831, a majority decision whereby leave was granted to apply for the resolution of what appeared to the applicants to be an ambiguous provision of the Constitution.

# C

# Constitutional Review

The disavowal of any law or decision of the Legislature as repugnant to or inconsistent with the Constitution under Article 179.2 is accompanied by corresponding mechanism for the constitutional review of such enactments established by Articles 140 and 144. Analogous mechanism is provided for by Article 146 with regard to action or inaction of organs and departments of the Executive in the exercise of executive or administrative authority. Moreover, Articles 137, 138, 141, 142 and 143 make provision for the review of the constitutionality of specific laws and decisions by reference to the Constitution or distinct provisions of it. Article 139, as earlier noted, makes provision for the resolution of conflicts or contests of power between organs or authorities of the Republic at the instance of the Executive or the Legislature or an organ or authority of the Republic involved in such a dispute. *1*

## I. Electoral Jurisdiction

The process for the election of the President of the Republic and the Vice- *2*
President of the Republic, members of the House of Representatives and other elected bodies is subject to review by the Supreme Constitutional Court[26] in exercise of jurisdiction vested in it by Articles 85 and 145.

[26] Later merged in the Supreme Court.

Electoral jurisdiction encompasses the review of the qualifications of candidates and the electoral process itself with a view to determining whether the election was held and conducted in accordance with the law and whether the result accurately reflects the choice of the electorate.

The holding of elections, the system of representation in the House of Representatives and the modalities of voting are not dealt with by the Constitution but are left to be regulated by law. An electoral law, as judicially noticed, must conform to constitutional norms including those enshrined in Article 31 assuring the right to vote to every citizen in every election held under the Constitution. Article 31 safeguarding a citizen's right to vote does not prescribe an age qualification for the exercise of this human right. Article 63.1 confines the right to vote to persons who have attained the age of 21. A law enacted by the House of Representatives lowering the age limit to 18 was declared unconstitutional in *President of the Republic v. House of Representatives (1985) 3 C.L.R. 2331 (P)*[27] on grounds of incompatibility with Article 63.1. While the Court recognized that the measure was politically desirable and socially beneficial, it rejected the plea that the law could be sustained in virtue of the law of necessity. As noticed in one of the judgments[28] given, "recourse to the law of necessity would be justified only if the electoral body would become inert without the participation of the new class of voters".

3 The Constitution does not prescribe any particular system of representation leaving the matter to be regulated by the Legislature. Any system may be adopted that does not thwart or distort the right of a person to participate in elections on an equal footing with everybody else. Implicit in the assured right to vote is the attachment of equal weight to every vote. The right of equality before and under the law guaranteed by Article 28 would not allow or permit any distinction or differentiation in this or any other respect.

The breadth of the electoral jurisdiction of the Supreme Court was examined in *Angelides v. Petas a.o. (1987) 1 C.L.R. 450 (FB)*.[29] The Court found that the electoral jurisdiction of the Supreme Court extends under the terms of Articles 85 and 145 to every issue relating to elections including the constitutionality of the provisions of the electoral law but not to matters following thereafter. Thus, in *President of the Republic v. House of*

---

[27] Judgments delivered by Triantafyllides P. and Pikis J.

[28] That of Pikis J.

[29] Judgment delivered by Triantafyllides P.

*Representatives (No. 1) (1999) 3 C.L.R. 735 (P)*[30] the Court declined jurisdiction to rule on the propriety of the action of a Representative crossing the line to join another parliamentary party. Consequently, the petition was dismissed as ill-founded. Assumption of jurisdiction on the subject would inevitably result in the issuing of directions affecting the functioning of the legislative body.

## II. Acts of the Attorney General

The Attorney General is an independent officer of the Republic holding office under the same terms and conditions as superior judges. The Constitution provides that he shall be the legal adviser of the President, the Vice-President and the Council of Ministers of the Republic. In addition, the Attorney General has overall responsibility for the prosecution of crime. Power vests in the holder of office to institute, conduct, take over and continue or discontinue criminal proceedings.[31] The office of the Attorney General and the powers vested in the holder were an important institutional safeguard for the establishment of the framework for the assurance of government under the law. *4*

Acts and omissions of the Attorney General[32] and the police authorities respecting the investigation and prosecution of crime are not subject to judicial review under Article 146.1; for the reason that acts of this nature are inextricably linked to the judicial process. Such control as may be exercised over acts in this sphere lies with the Judiciary the custodian of criminal jurisdiction.[33]

## III. Review of the Constitutionality of Laws and Decisions of the Legislature – Pre-Emptive and Remedial Control

Hereafter, we shall examine the principles governing judicial review of the constitutionality of laws and decisions envisaged by Articles 140 and 144. The jurisdiction of the Supreme Constitutional Court to pronounce on the *5*

---

30 Judgment delivered by Pikis P.

31 See Articles 112 and 113.

32 The legal adviser of the government trusted with power exercised in the public interest to conduct, take over, continue or discontinue proceedings at his discretion (Article 113 of the Constitution).

33 See inter alia Republic v. Zacharia 2 R.S.C.C. 1 and Xenofontos v. Republic 2 R.S.C.C. 89.

constitutionality of laws or decisions is confined to primary legislation and decisions of the House of Representatives submitted for promulgation under Article 52.

In a system of separation of powers, delegation of the exercise of power by one branch of the State to another is not feasible. Consequently, the power conferred by Article 54(g) on the Legislature to delegate authority to the Council of Ministers to make orders or regulations for "the carrying into effect of any law" may be regarded as a deviation, albeit constitutionally sanctioned, from the application of the principle of separation of powers. Authority on the part of the Executive to issue secondary or subsidiary legislation in the context of Article 54(g) was judicially recognized in the case of *The Police v. Theodoros Hondrou a.o. 3 R.S.C.C. 82.*[34] The Court explained that the fact that subsidiary legislation emanates from the Executive does not sap the act of its legislative attributes. Secondary legislation too must conform to the Constitution, but in this case only remedial or sequential constitutional review under Article 144 is possible.[35] Pre-emptive constitutional control under Article 140, on the other hand, is confined to laws and decisions of the House of Representatives.

6 Not only the constitutionality of subsidiary legislation but its conformity to the enabling law too may be tested in judicial proceedings. Secondary legislation must derive from the authorization given by law and be fashioned within its framework. Overstepping these limits will render subsidiary legislation ultra vires the law. As the Court noted in *Malachtou v. Attorney General (1981) 1 C.L.R. 543 (CA)*[36]: "The power for the enactment of subsidiary legislation must, in the nature of things, emanate strictly from the provisions of the enabling law". Elsewhere in its judgment the Court noted: "They cannot infer the existence of authority to legislate, other than that expressly conferred by law, and must therefore confine themselves within the four corners of the law".

7 The constitutionality of acts and decisions issued in the exercise of executive or administrative authority is reviewable in proceedings under Article 146.1. The same is true with regard to omissions occurring as a result of

[34] The judgment of the Court was read by Forsthoff P.

[35] In accordance with Article 186 the term "law" should be construed as meaning a law of the Republic.

[36] Judgment delivered by Pikis J.

failure to carry out a duty associated with the exercise of executive or administrative authority.

Omission to carry out a duty dictated by the Constitution renders it constitutionally objectionable. Acting within the Constitution and in accordance with its provisions is a prerequisite for the valid exercise of executive and administrative authority.

## IV. Raising Questions of Constitutionality

With the exception of the jurisdiction of courts under Article 188 to modify pre-independence legislation in a manner bringing it into accord with the Constitution, a species of original constitutional jurisdiction, a question of constitutionality of a law or decision must be duly raised and succinctly defined by a party to judicial proceedings disputing it. In the case of a reference of the constitutionality of a law or decision of the Legislature by the President of the Republic pursuant to Article 140, the very subject matter of the proceedings is the constitutionality of the law. The relevant Rules of Court[37] prescribing the form in which such reference should be raised require the specification of the contested part of the legislation and articulation of the reasons rendering it unconstitutional. *8*

In every other case, where the constitutionality of a law or decision is not the subject matter of the proceedings, issues of constitutionality must be specifically raised by juxtaposing the disputed provisions of a statute to the Article or Articles of the Constitution or the doctrine of separation of powers allegedly infringed thereby. *9*

In civil proceedings, an issue of constitutionality must be raised in the pleadings of the parties, that is in the written statement of the case of the plaintiff or the defendant. The response of the adversary to the issue must likewise be set out in that party's pleading. If not in the pleadings, the issue may be raised at a subsequent stage, again in writing, affording thereby an opportunity to the opposite party to respond thereto. This was declared to be the proper practice for raising questions of constitutionality of a law in civil proceedings in *The Improvement Board of Eylenja v. Andreas Constantinou (1967) 1 C.L.R. 167 (CA).*[38] In prescribing this practice the Court did not overlook that questions

[37] Rules of the Supreme Constitutional Court, 1962, and subsequent amendments.

[38] Judgment delivered by Josephides J.

relevant to the constitutionality of laws involve legal issues that are not, as opposed to material facts, ordinarily pleaded. Nonetheless, questions of constitutional importance are of especial significance and cannot be allowed to be raised in "an offhand way". In the subsequent case of *Istanbouli Brothers v. The Director of the Department of Customs and Excise (1986) 1 C.L.R. 465 (CA)*[39] the Court treated the practice approved in the above case as being "... more of a directive rather than laying down hard and fast rules to be followed at all times ..." emphasizing the legal nature of constitutional issues which are not as a rule the subject of pleading. The approach of the Court in the above decision met with the approval of the majority[40] in *Paporis v. National Bank of Greece (1986) 1 C.L.R. 578 (FB) (majority decision)*. The minority[41] took the view that "The solemnity of such issues makes necessary strict adherence to the aforementioned practice direction of the Supreme Court." The position was taken that in the absence of proper written elicitation of constitutional issues the Court should not "embark on their examination".

*10* In criminal proceedings there are no written pleadings for the definition of matters at issue other than the statement of the offence or offences; therefore a question of unconstitutionality of a law material for the determination of the subject matter of the proceedings must be raised orally at an appropriate stage of the trial; normally at the close of the case for the prosecution in the context of a submission of no case to answer, or at the end of the day in the final address of a party. A question of constitutionality of a law or decision of the House of Representatives may according to Article 144.1 be raised for the first time on appeal.

*11* Challenge to the constitutionality of a law does not suspend its application as noted in *A. Efthymiou Enterprise Ltd. a.o. v. Holy Archbishopric of Cyprus (1998) 1 C.L.R. 1596 (CA)*.[42] The Court will treat a law found to be unconstitutional as stillborn and consequently inapplicable to the determination of the case in hand. It does not, however, expunge the law from the statute book. The principle of binding precedent finding application in Cyprus along the same lines as in England[43] reduces in practice the importance of

---

[39] Judgment delivered by Triantafyllides P.

[40] Justices Loizou and Savvides who delivered separate concurring judgments.

[41] Judgment delivered by Pikis J.

[42] Judgment delivered by Pikis P.

[43] Republic v. D. Demetriades (1977) 3 C.L.R. 213; Mavrogenis v. House of Representatives a.o. (No. 3) (1996) 1 C.L.R. 315.

non-deletion of an enactment from the realm of the law. The House of Representatives does, as a rule, abrogate a law declared to be unconstitutional heeding the authoritative pronouncement of the Judiciary on the subject.

## V. Testing the Constitutionality of Laws – The Principles

Questions of constitutionality are decided *in abstracto* upon contrasting the impugned law with the provisions of the Constitution allegedly infringed thereby or the doctrine of separation of powers that earmarks the authority of state powers under the Constitution. As a rule, evidence is inadmissible as a means of disclosure of contradictions or inconsistencies between the law challenged and the relevant provisions of the Constitution. The incompatibility, if any, must emerge as a logical corollary of the process of comparison between them. However, if the implications of the law are not clear, evidence may be received to illuminate them shedding light thereby on its compatibility with the cited Article(s) of the Constitution or the doctrine of separation of powers (see *Mayor of Nicosia v. Cyprus Oil Industries Ltd. 2 R.S.C.C. 7*[44]; *Nicosia Police v. Evgenia Georghiou 4 R.S.C.C. 36*[45] and *Kyriakides (No. 1) v. Council of Registration of Architects and Civil Engineers (1965) 3 C.L.R. 151(SJ)*[46]). *12*

Examination of the constitutionality of a law or decision is strictly confined to the determination of their compatibility with the Constitution and the principle of separation of powers which underlies it. A law or decision will be declared unconstitutional if it is contrary to or inconsistent with one or more provisions of the Constitution. The decision in *President of the Republic v. House of Representatives (1994) 3 C.L.R. 64 (P) (majority decision)*[47] illustrates the distance the Court will keep from the utility or fruitfulness of the answer to a given question of constitutionality. In that case, the constitutionality of a law of limited duration was referred to the Supreme Court for its opinion under Article 140. By the time the proceedings were concluded the life of the law had expired. The Court did not refrain, though invited to, from resolving the questions of constitutionality raised explaining that its *13*

[44] The judgment of the Court was read by Forsthoff P.

[45] The judgment of the Court was read by Forsthoff P.

[46] Judgment delivered by Triantafyllides J.

[47] Majority judgment delivered by Pikis J., minority judgment delivered by Artemides J.

jurisdiction is limited to resolution of the issue of constitutionality without ponderation of the consequences. The decision is consonant with the settled principle of constitutional law that the jurisdiction of the Supreme Constitutional Court is confined to a review of the constitutionality of a law and not its aftereffects.

It is an axiom of constitutional law that upon constitutional review, the Court will not inquire into the wisdom of the law or the soundness of the policy of the legislator (see inter alia *Kyriakides v. Board of Registration of Architects and Civil Engineers (1966) 3 C.L.R. 640 (SJ)*[48]; *President of the Republic v. House of Representatives (1989) 3 C.L.R. 1931 (P) (majority judgment).*[49] Determination of the constitutionality of a law or decision submitted for promulgation is a pure question of law. The Court will not make a value judgment about the importance of the law or its desirability. The case is exemplified by the decision in *President of the Republic v. House of Representatives (1991) 3 C.L.R. 252 (P)*[50] where at issue was the constitutionality of a law depriving members of the coup d'état government of the right to become candidates for election to the House of Representatives. The qualifications for election to the House, comprehensively laid down in Article 64, do not stipulate for any such disqualification. What entails disqualification, according to the Constitution, is conviction for an offence involving dishonesty or moral turpitude. Members of the coup d'état government were not prosecuted save for the one who usurped the Office of President of the Republic. The Court held that the disqualification introduced by law could not be countenanced as it was inconsistent with Article 64. Conviction for an offence involving usurpation of state power, the Court pointed out, would involve moral turpitude leading to disqualification. Reprehensible as the conduct of such persons was, in the absence of conviction it provided no ground for disqualification. Disqualification was exhaustively defined in the Constitution.

*14* A finding of unconstitutionality of one or more sections of a law does not automatically render the law unconstitutional in its entirety. If the unconstitutional provisions can be severed from the rest of the law, only the part tainted with unconstitutionality will be disowned. The test of severability is

48 Judgment delivered by Josephides J.

49 The subject is addressed both in the majority judgment delivered by A. Loizou P. and the minority judgment delivered by Pikis J.

50 Concurring judgments as to the result delivered by A. Loizou P. and Pikis J.

an objective one revolving around the implications and impact of the unconstitutional provisions on the remaining part of the law. If the unconstitutional part is inextricable from the unobjectionable part of the law so that severance is impossible, the legislation will be declared unconstitutional in its entirety. The test of severability of the unconstitutional part from the rest of the law is the following: Does severance leave unaffected the nucleus of the law? If the answer is in the affirmative, severance will be approved. This was the test propounded in *President of the Republic v. House of Representatives (No. 1) (2000) 3 C.L.R. 157 (P)*[51] with regard to severability (see also *President of the Republic v. House of Representatives (No. 1) (2001) 3 C.L.R. 83 (P)*[52]). The Legislature is deemed to intend to exercise its legislative power within the framework of the Constitution. This presumption warrants the interpretation of an enactment in a manner reconciling it with the relevant constitutional provisions; provided always the wording of the law, read in context, allows such amenity. If not the law will be declared unconstitutional (see *Police v. Ekdotiki Eteria (1982) 2 C.L.R. 63 (FB)*[53]).

---

51 Judgment delivered by Pikis J.
52 Judgment delivered by Pikis P.
53 Judgments delivered by Pikis J., Triantafyllides P. and Loizou J.

# D

# Law of Necessity

## I. The Prelude to the Invocation of the Law of Necessity

Cyprus was inhabited by Greeks and Turks at the ratio of 82 percent and 18 percent respectively. This was approximately the make up of the population of Cyprus during British rule and at the time of independence.[54] Greeks and Turks were evenly spread throughout the island. The liberation struggle waged by the Greek Cypriots against the British occupation of the country[55] that took a dynamic form from the year 1955 created tension between the two communities. The Turkish Cypriots opposed the movement as well as the demand of the Greek Cypriots for the application of the principle of *1*

[54] The Greek community included the small Christian communities of Maronites, Aremenians and Latins making up approximately 2 percent of the population who opted to belong to the Greek community under the provisions of Article 2.3 of the Constitution.

[55] Earlier in 1954 Britain ruled out the exercise of the right to self-determination by the people of Cyprus. In a debate in Parliament on Cyprus (Constitutional Arrangements) held on 28th of July 1954, the Minister of State for Colonial Affairs Mr. Henry Hopkinson repeated five times that the question of sovereignty does not arise in the case of Cyprus explaining "that nothing less than continued sovereignty over this island can enable Britain to carry out her strategic obligations to Europe, the Mediterranean and the Middle East." (see Hansard, House of Commons Daily Debates, 28 July 1954, columns 504–514).

self-determination to the island that might predictably result in the choice of the majority of the people of the country to unite with Greece. The Turkish position was that colonial rule should continue insisting, with the support and encouragement of Turkey, that in the event of British withdrawal the island should be partitioned in order to accommodate in geographically separate areas the Greeks and Turks of Cyprus. Turkish Cypriots joined the colonial police force in increasing numbers combining with the British in the effort to suppress the uprising. The Zurich-London Agreements resulting in the settlement of the Cyprus problem and the declaration of the independence of the island[56] eased tensions between the two communities but did not eradicate them.

At the end of 1963, intercommunal strife erupted between the two communities with grave consequences for constitutional order. The strife continued in 1964. Following this upheaval, the President of the High Court (who under the Constitution shall be a neutral Judge not being "a subject or a citizen of the Republic or of the Kingdom of Greece or of the Republic of Turkey or of the United Kingdom and the Colonies"), a Canadian citizen, resigned in May 1964 rendering the High Court inactive, resulting in the paralysis of the Judiciary of Cyprus. The Supreme Constitutional Court was headless and incapable of functioning since April 1963 when the German President of the Court (likewise stipulated to be a neutral Judge under the Constitution as in the case of the High Court) went on holiday, resigning from his position with effect from the end of July of the same year. The Australian judge who was chosen to succeed him did not take up his appointment due to take effect in January 1964, seemingly owing to the upheaval in the country. Turkish Cypriots congregated in large numbers in areas assuring ethnic homogeneity preventing entry thereto to non-Turkish Cypriots while Turkish Cypriot officials of government from the Vice-President downwards withdrew from their positions and refused to participate in the exercise of state authority; the sole exception were the Turkish Cypriot Judges of the country who after a lull of a few months returned to their duties in June 1964.[57]

In a series of Resolutions[58] the Security Council of the United Nations, after taking stock of the anomalous situation in the island and the complaints of the Government of Cyprus that there was armed defiance of the

56 Two areas of Cyprus defined in Annex A of the Treaty of Establishment of Cyprus were retained by the United Kingdom as sovereign base areas used as military bases for the stationing of British troops in the island. Moreover, the British retained the right to use certain sites on the island for like purposes listed in Annex B, Part II of the Treaty of Establishment.

57 Turkish Cypriot Judges retired or withdrew from their positions in 1966.

58 S/RES/186 (1964) of 4 March 1964; S/RES/187 (1964) of 13 March 1964.

State by Turkish Cypriots, violations of sea and air space by Turkey and recurrent threats to invade the island, adopted measures to pacify the country by sending a United Nations Peacekeeping Force. In its unanimous resolution of 4 March 1964 (S/5575 or S/RES/186 (1964)) the Security Council asked the government of Cyprus "which has the responsibility for the maintenance and restoration of law and order, to take all additional measures necessary to stop violence and bloodshed in Cyprus".

The Judiciary and the State by and large were paralysed. Against this background the Courts of Justice (Miscellaneous Provisions) Law (L-33/64) was enacted to save the Judiciary from collapse, restore its functionality enabling it thereby to fulfil its constitutional mission. In the face of the inability of the Judiciary to operate and the absence of any real prospect of filling the gap left by the departure of the foreign Presidents of the two superior courts, provision was made for the fusion of the two courts of the land into the Supreme Court of Cyprus; trusted with the jurisdiction, competencies and powers of the two immobilized superior courts, into whose shoes it stepped. The Supreme Court would be composed of the Greek and Turkish Cypriot Judges of the Supreme Constitutional Court and the High Court. The first President of the Supreme Court would be the senior Judge of the higher Judiciary, namely Mr. Justice Zekia, a Turkish Cypriot, who took up the office of President of the Supreme Court in accordance with the law. Notwithstanding their unification, the separate jurisdictions and powers of the two courts reposed in the Supreme Court would be exercised within the framework of and in the manner ordained by the Constitution. There was neither amalgamation of jurisdictions nor alteration of the prerequisites for their invocation. The changes made mainly affected the exercise of *2*

a) the appellate jurisdiction, henceforth to be exercised by a bench composed of three Judges of the Supreme Court, unless otherwise directed by the plenum, and
b) the revisional jurisdiction under Article 146.1 assigned to a single judge subject to an appeal to the full bench; unless jurisdiction for the trial of a recourse was assumed from the outset by the Court en banc, in which case there would be no appeal.

The tumultuous events occurring at the end of 1963 spilling over into 1964 are recited in the preamble to the law L-33/64 as well as the necessity to provide the means for the sustenance of the judicial power, one of the pillars of the State. The measures adopted were stated to be temporary until a solution to the Cyprus problem was found.

## II. The Law of Necessity – the Principles

3 The constitutionality of law L-33/64 was tested before the Supreme Court in the case of *Attorney General v. Mustafa Ibrahim a.o. (1964) C.L.R. 195 (CA).*[59] The Court found the law to be justified in virtue of the law or doctrine of necessity. The Court took pains to explain the premises of the law of necessity and its limitations. The following principles emerge from the judgment in *Ibrahim* (supra):

1. The law of necessity inheres in every legal system. This is also implicit in the notion of the supremacy of the Constitution. The law of necessity is an ultimate norm of legal order, a defensive measure to save the State from petering out. It is a means to an end, not an end in itself. Dire need to save the State and its institutions, foremost constitutional order, is what legitimizes recourse to the law of necessity.
2. Recourse to the law of necessity is a last resort. No means must be available within the context of the Constitution to maintain constitutional order. Nothing short of necessity, in the extremity of the term, can justify the invocation of the doctrine of necessity.
3. The measures adopted must be exclusively directed towards underpinning constitutional order, filling the vacuum left by the necessitous circumstances of the country.
4. The object of the law of necessity is not to supplant but to safeguard constitutional order by such measures as are indispensable to enable the State and its institutions to function in accordance with the Constitution.
5. The bodies set up to substitute for public authorities that became inert owing to the emergency confronting the country must have the attributes of the constitutional organs they substitute for and must, moreover, operate within the framework and parameters of their authority under the Constitution.
6. The law of necessity is per se a temporary measure that cannot outlast chronologically the emergency that necessitated recourse to it. The prerequisites for valid invocation of the doctrine of necessity are

[59] Elaborate judgments were delivered by each one of the three members of the Court nominated to hear the appeal from the District Court – Justices Vassiliades, Triantafyllides and Josephides. In their judgments extensive reference is made to the doctrine of the law of necessity as judicially understood and applied and discussed by legal scholars in the United States (reserve power), France (exceptional circumstances) England, Greece and Italy.

> defined as follows in one of the judgments[60] of the Supreme Court in *Ibrahim*: "a) an imperative and inevitable necessity or exceptional circumstances; b) no other remedy to apply; c) the measure taken must be proportionate to the necessity; and d) it must be of a temporary character limited to the duration of the exceptional circumstances."

In another judgment[61] of the Supreme Court in *Ibrahim* (supra), the law or doctrine of necessity is parallelised to the defence of necessity as understood and applied under English criminal law. Inasmuch as a person, to avert imminent threat to life may take measures unwarranted by the law preventing thereby the occurrence of a greater evil, so can a State take extralegal measures to avert imminent threats to its existence; the greater evil being the collapse of the State.

The expectation for the restoration of constitutional order did not materialize; on the contrary, the situation deteriorated as a result of two events that shook the foundations of the country and put to peril the very being of its inhabitants. In July 1974, a coup d'état was staged by the military junta that ruled Greece resulting in the overthrowing of the democratically elected government of Cyprus. A puppet government assumed power under the strong arm of the military. Five days later, another guarantor power of Cyprus' independence, Turkey, invaded the island with a massive force resulting in the occupation of part of the country. Soon after (two to three days later), the coup government in Cyprus as well as the government of the military junta in Greece collapsed, opening the way for the restoration of democracy in Greece and the restoration of the legitimate government in Cyprus. Less than a month later, Turkey mounted a second and far more deadly military operation designed to expand Turkish hold over the island, ending with the military occupation of nearly 40 percent of the country. This development made the claim of Turkey that it invaded the island in order to restore constitutional order appear as a mere pretext. The vast majority of the population residing in the occupied area were Greek Cypriots. As a consequence of the invasion and occupation, they were ousted from their homes and ancestral land, taking refuge in the unoccupied part of Cyprus. The circumstances of their uprootal, and the coercive means used by the occupying power to achieve this and the violation of the fundamental human rights and liberties of citizens of Cyprus inherent therewith and incidental thereto are chronicled in 4

[60] That of Josephides J., page 265.
[61] That of Vassiliades J.

the decisions of the European Commission on Human Rights to which Cyprus had recourse.[62] Meantime, the Turkish Cypriot population residing in the remaining part of the island moved and was settled in the occupied area. In the process of occupation, thousands of Turks from mainland Turkey came over and were aided to settle in the occupied part of Cyprus, producing sizeable demographic changes in the complexion of the population of the island. Thereafter, on 15th November 1983, the Turkish Cypriot leadership, seemingly with the acquiescence and connivance of Turkey, proclaimed the occupied part to be an independent state. The Security Council denounced the proclamation of an independent state;[63] no country other than Turkey recognized it. In *Case of Loizidou v. Turkey Application No. 15318/89, 18th December 1996* the European Court of Human Rights acknowledged that the Northern part of Cyprus is under Turkish occupation, adjudging Turkey to pay compensation to the applicant, a Greek Cypriot from an occupied area, for depriving her of the right to property, its enjoyment and possession. A similar finding was made and the juridical implications of Turkish occupation of a part of Cyprus were likewise depicted in a subsequent recourse of Cyprus against Turkey before the European Court of Human Rights (see *Case of Cyprus v. Turkey Application No. 25781/94, 10th May 2001*).[64]

5 Despite the calamity that befell Cyprus, leaving thousands of people homeless and largely unemployed, none of the fundamental rights and liberties of the individual were suspended nor was a state of emergency declared. The Constitution permits the suspension of certain Articles of the Constitution[65] "in case of war or other public danger threatening the life of the Republic or any part thereof". The right to declare a state of emergency vests in the Council of Ministers[66] subject to confirmation by the House of Representatives. A state of emergency shall come to an end after two months unless prolonged by a new decision of the Council of Ministers and legislative

[62] Cyprus against Turkey, Application No. 6780/74, 6950/75, 26 May 1975, Report of Strasbourg Commission, 1976 – published on 31st August 1979 (D.H. (79)); Report of European Commission on Human Rights of 4th October 1983 – published on 2nd April 1992 – D.H. (92) – Conclusions reported in E.H.R.R. 15 (1992) 509511; Report YB – 1996 p. 130 to 166.

[63] See Security Council Resolution S/RES/541 (1983), 18 November 1983.

[64] See also the last decision of the European Court of Human Rights on the subject: Case of Xenides-Arestis v. Turkey (Application No. 46347/99, 22nd December 2005).

[65] Provision to that effect is made in Articles 182, 183 and 184 of the Constitution.

[66] Subject to a veto power of the President and Vice-President of the Republic.

confirmation. It must be noted that Articles of the Constitution which have been incorporated from the Zurich Agreement set out in Annex III of the Constitution cannot be suspended. Moreover, only some of the fundamental rights of the individual can be suspended, those specified in Article 183.2.[67] The law of necessity continued to provide the basis for the rule of the country with the courts ever watchful to see that its bounds were not transgressed. The Supreme Court[68] underlined, time and again, that the doctrine of necessity provides no warrant for supplanting or bypassing constitutional order. Its invocation must be confined to acts absolutely necessary to enable the State to function under the Constitution, the supreme law of the land.

The following extract from one of the judgments of the Supreme Court in *Aloupas v. National Bank of Greece (1983) 1 C.L.R. 55 (FB)*[69], where the principles of the law of necessity came under review, is indicative of the judicial approach to the subject:

> The rule of law does not abate in an emergency subject to the qualification that necessity creates a valid juridical basis for legal action. Legislative measures are subject to judicial control. The Judiciary is charged to ensure that the measures taken are a genuine response to a necessity and, further, that they go no further than the necessity warrants.

The role of the Judiciary as the guardian of the rule of law becomes greater still in an emergency. The doctrine of necessity forfeits its legal justification if its constraints are loosened and its limitations transgressed.[70] The measures taken in virtue of necessity must be absolutely necessary for the sustenance of constitutional order. They must be strictly proportionate to the exigencies of necessity. This is a common and recurring theme of the case law of the Supreme Court.

---

67 "Article 7, only in so far as it relates to death inflicted by a permissible act of war, Article 10, paragraphs 2 and 3; Article 11; Article 13; Article 16; Article 17; Article 19; Article 21; Article 23, paragraph 8, sub-paragraph (d); Article 25 and Article 27."

68 See inter alia: Messaritou v. The Cyprus Broadcasting Corporation (1972) 3 C.L.R. 100; Solomou v. Republic (1984) 3 C.L.R. 533; Makrides a.o. v. Republic (1984) 3 C.L.R. 677; Petroudes v. E.A.C. (1985) 3 C.L.R. 2245.

69 Extract from judgment of Pikis J. at page 78; judgments were also delivered by Triantafyllides P. and Hadjianastassiou J.

70 See inter alia Republic v Nicolaos Sampson (1977) 2 C.L.R. 1; Apostolides a.o. v. Republic (1982) 3 C.L.R. 928; President of the Republic v. House of Representatives (1991) 3 C.L.R. 252.

6 The Judiciary is the final arbiter of the existence of necessity and the judge of the justification of measures taken to address it. The case of *Pastellopoulos v. Republic (1985) 2 C.L.R. 165 (FB) (majority decision)*[71] is to the point: whereas necessity arising from attacks of Turkey against the island[72] and her repeated threats to invade it justified the establishment of a national guard for the defence of the country, not foreseen in the Constitution, no justification could be found for the establishment of a Military Court outside constitutional norms governing the composition of a judicial body. At issue was the constitutionality of the provisions of the Military and Criminal Procedure Code envisaging the appointment of the President of the Military Court by the Council of Ministers and members of it by the Commander of the force. The Supreme Court denounced this part of the law as unconstitutional on account of its incompatibility with Article 157.2 entrusting judicial appointments to every inferior court of law exclusively to the Judiciary. Moreover, the relevant provisions of the Code fell foul of the provisions of Article 30.2 in that the composition of the court did not have, on account of the appointment of its judges by the Executive, the attributes of "independence" and "impartiality".

7 The application of the doctrine of necessity as judicially acknowledged is subject to one other proviso. Organs set up to substitute for organs that ceased to be functional, owing to the emergency, must have the attributes of the organs they replace. Furthermore, they must be invested with the same jurisdiction, competencies and powers and operate within the framework prescribed by the Constitution. This principle was given effect to in *Kyriacou v. The Republic (1987) 3 C.L.R. 1130 (SJ)*[73], where Section 4(3) of the Public Service Law (L-33/67) was declared to be unconstitutional. On the other hand, the setting up of a Public Service Commission to substitute for the corresponding constitutional body that ceased to function owing to the withdrawal of its Turkish Cypriot members was justified by the law of necessity. The terms of service of members of it could not be other than those envisaged by the relevant provisions of the Constitution. Consequently, Section 4(3) of the law that gave power to the President to dismiss members

---

[71] Majority judgment delivered by Styliades J., minority judgment delivered by A. Loizou J.

[72] See inter alia Security Council Resolution S/RES/193 (1964), 9 August 1964, ordering Turkey to stop instantly the bombardment of and the use of military force of any kind against Cyprus appealing at the same time to the government of Cyprus to order the armed forces under its control to cease firing immediately.

[73] Judgment delivered by Pikis J.

of the Commission was found to be unconstitutional for inconsistency with Article 124.5 providing that members of the Commission "shall not be removed from office except on like grounds and in a like manner as Judges of the High Court".[74] Article 153.8 provides that removal of Judges on grounds of misconduct or inability to perform their duties can only be sanctioned by a judicial council in proceedings of a judicial nature.

The same point, i.e. that bodies set up to substitute for bodies envisaged by the Constitution should have the same attributes as the latter, is made in *Hadjidemetriou v. CTO (1986) 3 C.L.R. 1956 (SJ)*[75] reversed on appeal (see *CTO v. Hadjidemetriou (1987) 3 C.L.R. 780 (FB)*[76]) but without doubting the validity of the aforementioned principle.

In the cases of *Orphanides a.o. v. Republic (1992) 3 C.L.R. 44 (FB)*[77] and *Attorney General v. Artemiou (1991) 2 C.L.R. 150 (FB)*[78] the Court made a thorough analysis of the competence, jurisdiction and powers of the Supreme Court concluding that they derive solely and exclusively from the Constitution, identical to those vested in the two superior courts into whose shoes the Supreme Court stepped. Furthermore, the separateness of the competencies, jurisdiction, and powers of the two superior courts must be observed and procedurally heeded all the way along the lines drawn by the Constitution and be exercised within the framework envisaged therein. 8

The law of necessity as expounded in *Ibrahim* (supra) and the principles expressed therein were treated by the Supreme Court of Canada as an accurate reflection of the principles of the law of necessity in the case of *Languages Rights under the Manitoba Act 1870 (1985) 19 D.L.R. (4th)1.*[79] After review of international jurisprudence, the Supreme Court of Canada 9

[74] Dicta of the Supreme Court in the earlier decisions of Republic v. Louca a.o. (1984) 3 C.L.R. 241 (FB) and Josephides v. The Republic (1986) 3 C.L.R. 111 highlighted the apparent inconsistency of Section 4 (3) of the law with Article 124.5 of the Constitution. Eventually, Section 4(3) was repealed and replaced by a provision compatible with the Constitution.

[75] Judgment delivered by Pikis J.

[76] Judgment delivered by Triantafyllides P.

[77] Judgment delivered by Pikis J.

[78] Judgment delivered by Pikis J.

[79] On the subject of the law of necessity see also Madzimbamuto v. Lardner-Burke (1968) 3 All E.R. 561 (P.C.); Pakistan v. Tamizuddin Khan P.L.R. 1956 W.P. 306; Special Ref. 1 of 1955, P.L.R. 1956 W.P. 598; Texas v. White, 74 U.S. 700, 19 L. Ed. 227 (1869); Horn v. Lockhart, 84 U.S. 570, 21 L. Ed. 657 (1873); Baldy v. Hunter, 171 U.S. 388, 43 L. Ed. 208 (1898).

depicted the principles underlying the law of necessity in these terms: "the courts will recognize unconstitutional enactments as valid where a failure to do so would lead to legal chaos and thus violate the constitutional requirement of the rule of law"; adding that this principle is well-expressed in the following extract from the judgment of Mr. Justice Triantafyllides in *Ibrahim*, supra, at p. 237:

> If the position was that the administration of justice and the preservation of the rule of law and order in the State could no longer be secured in a manner which would not be inconsistent with the constitution, a constitution under which the sovereign will of the people could not be expressed so as to regulate through an amendment of the fundamental law such a situation, then the House of Representatives, elected by the people, should be empowered to take such necessary steps as are warranted, by the doctrine of necessity, in the exigencies of the situation. Otherwise the absurd corollary would have been entailed *viz.* that a State, and the people, should be allowed to perish for the sake of the constitution; on the contrary a constitution should exist for the preservation of the State and the welfare of the people.

*10* In 1987, the Foreign Affairs Committee of the House of Commons of the United Kingdom examined whether Cyprus operated in accordance with the Constitution of the country. The government of Cyprus was invited to make its representations on the matter. Addressing the subject, the government of Cyprus submitted a document explaining the background to the adoption of the law of necessity and its application as it emerges from the case law of the Supreme Court. The outcome of the inquiry is reflected in the following statement of Undersecretary Baroness Young: "We have not accepted that the Constitution is not still in force".[80]

## III. The Law of Necessity and Amenity to Amend the Constitution

*11* An issue that divided judicial opinion was whether the law of necessity could provide justification for the amendment of the Constitution in face of pressing need to change what were perceived to be anachronistic provisions of it. In *President of the Republic v. House of Representatives (1986)*

---

[80] Referred to in the judgment of Pikis J. in Nicolaou a.o. v. Nicolaou a.o. (No. 2) (1992) 1 C.L.R. 1338, 1402–1405.

*3 C.L.R. 1439 (P)*,[81] the first case where such an issue came up for consideration, the majority of the Supreme Court opined that the law of necessity might provide justification for such a course but only in a case where extraordinary reasons dictated it; such as would outweigh the dominant need not to amend the Constitution of the polity of Cyprus in any matter affecting both communities; hence, the amendment made was declared to be unconstitutional in the absence of compelling reasons justifying such a course. The minority likewise denounced the law as unconstitutional but for wholly different reasons. In their view the law of necessity could in no circumstances provide justification for the amendment of the Constitution. Necessity to resort to extralegal measures derives, it was stressed, from inability to amend the Constitution. If amenity to do so does exist, recourse to the law of necessity would be superfluous and in fact wrong because measures would be taken outside the realm of the law, when their adoption was feasible within its context. In the opinion of the minority, acknowledgment of power to amend the Constitution under the doctrine of necessity is a contradiction in terms. Acts legitimized by the doctrine of necessity are per se temporary, whereas a change of the Constitution aims to serve the diachronic needs of the State.

In the case of *Nicolaou a.o. v. Nicolaou a.o. (No. 2) (1992) 1 C.L.R. 1338 (P)* *12*
the Supreme Court[82] was required to determine the constitutionality of L-95/89 amending Article 111 that entrusted matters of personal status (betrothal, marriage, divorce, nullity of marriage, judicial separation, restitution of conjugal rights) and family relations other than legitimation by order of the court or adoption of members of the Greek Orthodox church and other Christian denominations to the corresponding ecclesiastical authorities. By the amendment, jurisdiction on the aforesaid matters would vest in the Family Courts to be established by law.[83] The Court was equally divided as to the feasibility of amending the Constitution by reference to the law of necessity. Five of the ten members of the Court decided that the law could be justified under the law of necessity failing which the State would be deprived of the means to address vital issues affecting the well-being of

[81] Majority judgment with regard to the reasoning delivered by Triantafyllides P., minority judgment delivered by Pikis J.

[82] Composition: ten Judges.

[83] The reasons in support of the constitutionality of the law were given by Stylianides J. and Poyialjis J. and those for the opposite view by Pikis J. and Nikitas J.

society. The power to review the Constitution, when necessary, should not be denied to the people even in an emergency. The other five Judges were of the opinion that the amendment of the Constitution is not possible under the law of necessity. The very essence of the law of necessity derives from inability to change the Constitution whereupon justification is provided for taking measures to address perils posed to the cohesion of the State. It is this necessity that may legitimize measures unwarranted by law with a view to sustaining constitutional order. The equal division of the Court brought into play the presumption of constitutionality saving the law from doom.

13 In *Angelides v. Peta a.o. (1988) 1 C.L.R. 173 (FB) (majority decision)*[84] the Court was again divided as to the constitutionality of a law (L-95/46) making provision for the filling of vacant positions in the House of Representatives in a manner other than through a by-election as envisioned in Article 66.2. The majority, four of the seven members of the Court, held that inasmuch as the proportional system of representation establishes the order of success of the candidates of each party, in case of a vacancy the seat may justifiably be filled by the candidate next in the order of success at the general election, obviating thereby the need for a by-election. In other words, the general election foreshadows the filling of vacancies. Consequently, the relevant law that envisaged such a process of succession was not incompatible with Article 66.2 stipulating for the holding of a by-election to fill a seat in the House of Representatives that became vacant.

The position of the minority was founded on

a) the clear provisions of Article 66.2 laying down in mandatory terms that a by-election shall be held to fill a vacancy occurring in the House of Representatives,[85] and
b) the previous decision of the Supreme Court on the subject where the attempt to amend the Constitution in order to achieve the same objective was rejected as unconstitutional.

The same question came up for consideration some eight years later in *Mavrogenis v. House of Representatives a.o. (No. 3) (1996) 1 C.L.R. 315 (P) (majority decision)*.[86] The Court was asked to depart from the ratio of the case

[84] Majority judgment delivered by Triantafyllides P; minority judgment delivered by Pikis J.
[85] President of the Republic v. House of Representatives (1986) 3 C.L.R. 1439.
[86] Majority judgment delivered by Pikis P; minority judgments delivered by Artemides J. and Nicolaou J.

of *Angelides* (supra) on the ground that the decision was manifestly wrong, founded on a principle contradictory to the law of necessity. The Supreme Court examined at length the principles governing the application of the rule of binding precedent that finds application in Cyprus along the corresponding principles of English jurisprudence and the circumstances where departure from it may be justified. The Court concluded by majority that the case of *Angelides* (supra) had been wrongly decided. Disinclined as the Court is to depart from judicial precedent, it may or, more accurately, it should do so if it is found that it rests on an incontrovertibly wrong principle. The doctrine of necessity, the Court reaffirmed, provided no ground for sidelining the Constitution, no matter how salutary the reasons warranting the legislative measures taken may be. The Court rejected the submission to give to its decision prospective effect, leaving intact whatever had been unconstitutionally done. The Court drew attention to the supremacy of the Constitution and the prohibition of any law, act or decision contrary to its provisions, a fact that leaves no room for the sufferance of unconstitutional action. In *Republic v. Yiallourou (1995) 3 C.L.R. 363 (FB)*[87] the Court acknowledged that freedom to depart from a judicial precedent is greater if the principle adopted therein comes into conflict with a fundamental constitutional principle such as the doctrine of separation of powers. The minority adopted the principles earlier espoused in *Angelides* (supra).

Following the decision in *Mavrogenis* (supra), the House of Representatives proceeded with the amendment of Article 66.2 so as to accommodate succession to vacant seats in the House of Representatives by the candidate next in line of success at the last general election to the Representative of the party to which the vacant seat belonged. The constitutionality of the law came up for consideration in *Koulounti a.o. v. House of Representatives a.o. (1997) 1 C.L.R. 1026 (P)*[88]. The majority upheld the constitutionality of the law along the principles espoused by one part of the Court in *Nicolaou* (supra). The minority adhered to the views of the other part of the Court again in the case of *Nicolaou*. What may be of interest to note is that no other amendment to the Constitution was sought since.

---

[87] Judgment delivered by Pikis P.

[88] Majority judgments delivered by Justices Nikolaides, Artemides, Artemis, Nicolaou and Kronides; minority judgments delivered by Pikis P. and Justices Konstantinides and Kallis.

# E

# Human Rights

## I. Constitutional Guarantee of Human Rights

The fundamental rights and liberties of the individual aptly known as human rights are by and large entrenched in the Constitution of the Republic of Cyprus. Their interpretation, range of application and impact on the legal order of the country have attracted a voluminous body of case law. 1

To begin, legislation antedating the Constitution had to be brought into conformity with human rights. The concept of guaranteed rights and liberties had no antecedent in English law, the law applicable at the time of independence. Safeguarded rights are understood as rights that cannot be taken away, set aside or modified by statutory law. The fundamental principle of English constitutional law is that Parliament is supreme, empowered to legislate on any matter without fetter including the conferment, the abridgment or the taking away of rights. The only principle mitigating the rigour of this rule is that Parliament is presumed not to intend a change of the common law, historically the repository of the freedoms and liberties of the individual in England; a presumption that may be displaced by the clear wording of statutory law to the contrary.

Constitutionalism, the process whereby the legitimacy of statutory law is tested by reference to the higher order of a Constitution, is unknown to English law. Guaranteed rights and the compatibility of legislation with a superior legal order established by the Constitution were new to Cyprus 2 law. The principle of institutional separation of powers underlying the Cyprus Constitution was yet another novelty of the nascent legal order. The notions implicit in entrenched rights, the sphere of their application and their implications on the legal order of the country were explored to great lengths by the case law of the Supreme Court. In the process, legislation was tested with a view to determining its compatibility with the Constitution, both pre-emptively by a reference of the President or Vice-President before promulgation of the impugned law and more so sequentially or remedially in the context of judicial proceedings involving the application of the contested legislation. In *The Board for Registration of Architects & Civil Engineers v. Christodoulos Kyriakides (1966) 3 C.L.R. 640 (FB)*[83] the Court subscribed to the position that the review of the constitutionality of a statute is governed "by certain well established principles" one of them being that a law enacted by the Legislature is presumed to be constitutional, described as "a precautionary rule". The presumption carries little weight in the case of laws purporting to limit or abridge human rights as the Court affirmed in *President of the Republic v. House of Representatives (2000) 3 C.L.R. 238 (P)*.[84] It goes no further than establishing the bona fida intention of the Legislature to regulate a given matter. The practical significance of the presumption of constitutionality is that the Court will not examine, on its own motion, the constitutionality of a law enacted by the House of Representatives. An issue of constitutionality must be specifically raised by either or both parties to judicial proceedings and be succinctly defined before the Court adverts to it; subject always to the proviso that determination of the constitutional issue is material for the outcome of the case.

The presumption of constitutionality has no application to preemptive constitutional control where the very subject matter of the proceedings is the constitutionality of the law to be. The proceedings affect the genesis of the enactment prohibited to be anything other than in full accord with the Constitution (Article 179.2).

3 The charter of human rights enshrined in the Constitution is modelled on the European Convention on Human Rights[85] save that it is wider in scope

[83] Judgment delivered by Josephides J.

[84] Judgment delivered by Pikis P. reflecting the reasoning of the majority and concurring judgment delivered by Nicolaou J. reflecting the reasoning of the minority.

[85] Convention for the Protection of Human Rights and Fundamental Freedoms, 4 November 1950 as amended by Protocol No. 11, with Protocol Nos. 1, 4, 6, 7, 12 and 13, 213 United Nations Treaty Series 2889.

and less amenable to limitation or restriction of guaranteed rights. To give but few examples, the right to equality embodied in Article 28 goes beyond assuring enjoyment of human rights without discrimination, the subject of Article 14 of the European Convention on Human Rights, by positively guaranteeing equality under the law, before the law and equality of treatment by every authority of the State. Article 30.3[86] confers by and large upon litigants in every judicial proceeding the rights acknowledged to the accused by Article 6.3 of the European Convention on Human Rights, also guaranteed by Article 12.5[87] of the Constitution. I do not overlook that the case law of the European Court of Human Rights has in essence acknowledged to every litigant the rights conferred by Article 6.3 of the Convention notwithstanding the absence of express provision to that end, treating such rights as implicit in the notion of a fair trial guaranteed by Article 6.1 of the Convention (see inter alia *Case of Delcourt v. Belgium Application No. 2689/65, 17th January 1970*; *Case of Golder v. The United Kingdom Application No. 4451/70, 21st February 1975* and *Case of Albert and Le Compte v. Belgium Application No. 7299/75, 7496/76, 10th February 1983.* The liberty to practise any profession or to carry on any occupation, trade or business, the freedom to enter into any contract as well as many of the rights introduced by Protocols to the European Convention on Human Rights such as the right to property[88] were comprehensively incorporated into the constitutional charter of human rights.

Like Article 18 of the European Convention, the Cyprus Constitution provides that human rights cannot be limited except for a purpose specifically *4*

[86] It states: Every person has the right a) to be informed of the reasons why he is required to appear before the court; b) to present his case before the court and to have sufficient time necessary for its preparation; c) to adduce or cause to be adduced his evidence and to examine witnesses according to law; d) to have a lawyer of his own choice and to have free legal assistance where the interests of justice so require and as provided by law; e) to have free assistance of an interpreter if he cannot understand or speak the language used in court.

[87] It states: Every person charged with an offence has the following minimum rights: a) to be informed promptly and in a language which he understands and in detail of the nature and grounds of the charge preferred against him; b) to have adequate time and facilities for the preparation of his defence; c) to defend himself in person or through a lawyer of his own choosing or, if he has no sufficient means to pay for legal assistance, to be given free legal assistance when the interests of justice so require; d) to examine or have examined witnesses against him and to obtain the attendance and examination of witnesses on his behalf under the same conditions as witnesses against him; e) to have the free assistance of an interpreter if he cannot understand or speak the language used in court.

[88] Protocol 1 to the European Convention on Human Rights (Paris, 20 March 1952).

prescribed by the Constitution. Provision to that effect is made in Article 33.1. Paragraph 2 of the same Article adds that provisions relating to limitations or restrictions of protected human rights "shall be applied strictly", justifying a restrictive rather than an expansive interpretation of the causes in respect of which restrictions or limitations are permissible. Article 34 provides that nothing should be suffered involving

a) "the distraction of any of the rights or liberties set forth in Part II of the Constitutions" or
b) their limitation "to a greater extent than is provided for therein".

It is implicit in the concept of human rights that they should be exercised without detriment to the corresponding rights of others. Each person is entitled to the same rights as others, referable to human identity. Their rights coexist. Human rights must be enjoyed and exercised by a person in parallel to the enjoyment and exercise of the same rights by fellow human beings. This is a definitive element of the parameters of human rights. Article 35 imposes a positive obligation upon each one of the three powers of the State to ensure the effective application of human rights in the sphere of their respective competences. The unabating duty of every authority to protect within its domain human rights was emphasized in *Fakontis v. Republic (1987) 3 C.L.R. 557 (SJ)*.[89]

5 The European Convention on Human Rights[90] too was adopted and made part of Cyprus domestic law by law L-39/62 ratifying the Convention. Likewise, the International Covenant on Civil and Political Rights and the International Covenant on Economic, Social and Cultural Rights of 16 December 1966[91] were incorporated into municipal law by Ratification Law L-14/69. It must be explained that the Constitution of Cyprus adopts the monistic theory of incorporation of international treaties, conventions, agreements and covenants into domestic law. Self-executory provisions of treaties, conventions and international agreements duly ratified confer rights and impose liabilities without need arising to include their provisions into a separate enactment (see *Malachtou v. Armefti a.o. (1987) 1 C.L.R.*

[89] Judgment delivered by Pikis J.

[90] Convention for the Protection of Human Rights and Fundamental Freedoms, 4 November 1950 as amended by Protocol No. 11, with Protocol Nos. 1, 4, 6, 7, 12, and 13, 213 United Nations Treaty Series 2889.

[91] 999 United Nations Treaty Series 14668.

*207 (FB)*[92]). Article 169 stipulates that such international instruments, satisfying the principle of mutuality, shall have superior force to municipal law; their provisions prevailing in the event of conflict between the two. In terms of the hierarchy of laws, international treaties, agreements, covenants and conventions duly ratified rank next to the Constitution but unlike the Constitution they may be repealed without constitutional constraint. Any limitations as there may be to the repeal or revision of a treaty, convention or international agreement derive from international law.

The rights guaranteed by the aforementioned two important international instruments on human rights largely coincide with the provisions of the Constitution but they are not identical. Law L-14/69 guarantees for example a right to appeal against conviction and sentence in criminal cases (see Section 14(5)), a right not safeguarded by the Constitution. Article 25 of The Courts of Justice Law (L-14/60) enacted shortly after independence in 1960, confers on the accused a right to appeal against both conviction and sentence. Decisions of civil courts may likewise be the subject of an appeal at the instance of an aggrieved party. The Constitution, it may be said, does not assure a right of appeal against judgments of first instance courts.

## II. The Decision in Police v. Georghiades

The leading authority on the nature, scope and range of application of human rights is the case of *Police v. Georghiades (1983) 2 C.L.R. 33 (FB)*. At issue was the admissibility of a tape, recording the conversation between a psychologist and his client in the course of psychological examination, made without the knowledge and consent of the interlocutors. The object of the examination was to assess the psychological effects produced upon the client by injuries suffered in a road accident, compensation for which was the subject of a pending civil suit. The tape was submitted as evidence in criminal proceedings against the psychologist for purgery, the case for the prosecution being that he gave false testimony in his evidence before the civil court respecting the condition of the client. The content of the tape was meant to prove the falsity of his testimony. The accused objected to the production of the tape on the ground that the evidence had been obtained in breach of his right to privacy safeguarded by Article 15.1[93] (corresponding to Article 8 of *6*

[92] Judgments delivered by all five members of the Court; Triantafyllides P. and Justices, A. Loizou, Loris, Stylianiades and Pikis.

[93] It states: Every person has the right to respect for his private and family life.

the European Convention on Human Rights). The case for the prosecution was that the evidence, even if found to have been collected in violation of the right of the accused to privacy, was nonetheless admissible under the common law rule reflected in the English case of *R. v. Sang (1979) 2 All E.R. 1222 (H.L.)* acknowledging residual discretion to the court to admit evidence obtained by improper means. The trial court reserved, by way of case stated, the constitutional issue raised for consideration by the Supreme Court. The Supreme Court adverted to the nature of human rights, their application and the consequences of their breach. It concluded that the tape was inadmissible in evidence and with that advice sent the case back to the trial court. The decision of the Supreme Court was unanimous as to the inadmissibility of the tape in evidence. A number of judgments were given by members of the Court,[94] coinciding in essence in their approach to human rights and the consequences of their breach, wherefrom the following principles emerge:

a) Human rights reflect the attributes of man; they are inalienable, apt to be asserted against the State and fellow human beings. Respect for them is owed by the State as well as everybody else. They are universal in character. They operate *erga omnes*, horizontally across the social board.
b) Human nature is the denominator of human rights. They inhere in every person as an attribute of human existence. A corresponding duty is cast upon everyone, the State as well as everybody else, to respect them. In one of the judgments reference is made to Lord Mansfield's command in *Somerset v. Stewart (1772) 1 Loffit 1–19* to let free a black man chained on a ship anchored at an English port proclaiming that the air of England is too pure to admit such pollution.[95] In *Andreas Demosthenous (1967) 1 C.L.R. 186 (SJ)*[96] the Court issued a writ of *habeas corpus ad subjiciendum* directing the master of a ship to release a sailor from captivity.
c) Evidence obtained in breach of human rights is inadmissible in all circumstances, a fact consistent with the duty of every authority to ensure their effective application. It transpires from the tenor of the judgments given that admitting evidence in breach of human rights would tear their fabric.

---

[94] Judgments delivered by Triantafyllides P., Stylianides J. and Pikis J. Justices Hadjianastassiou and Loris espoused the reasoning of the judgment of Pikis J. and Justice Malachtos the reasoning of Triantafyllides P.

[95] It is tempting to remark that the air in some British colonies must have been sufficiently polluted to accommodate or suffer slavery.

[96] Judgment delivered by Hadjianastassiou J.

Citation of passages from one of the judgments of the Court[97] are characteristic of the approach of the Court to human rights and the consequences of their breach:

> On a consideration of the objects of Part II of the Constitution, the character of the rights entrenched therein and, the background thereto, outlined in this judgment, I am of the opinion that the basic rights safeguarded in this part of the Constitution, those referring to fundamental freedoms and liberties, are inalienable and inhere in man at all times, to be enjoyed and exercised under constitutional protection. Interference by anyone, be it the State or an individual, is unconstitutional and, a right vests thereupon in the victim to invoke constitutional, as well as municipal, law remedies for the vindication of his rights.

Subsequent judicial decisions stress that to be admissible both the provenance and the content of the evidence must be free of human rights violations. Evidence must be untainted by breaches or disregard of human rights. In *Merthodja v. Police (1987) 2 C.L.R. 227 (CA)*[98] the confession of a person in custody was declared to be inadmissible on account of the fact that the confessor was illegally detained at the time he made the statement. Consequently, his detention violated the fundamental right embodied in Article 11 that no one's liberty should be fettered except on the strength of express judicial authorization. Breach of the right invalidated every act sequential to his illegal detention. In the same spirit, it was decided in *Parpas v. Republic (1988) 2 C.L.R. 5 (CA)*[99] that the detention of a person for ulterior purposes, i.e. for purposes other than those for which detention was authorised, rendered his statement to the police inadmissible. The detention of the accused secured for a purpose other than the one for which it was sought rendered the specimens of his handwriting obtained during his detention inadmissible in evidence on charges of forgery. Article 11.6[100] 7

---

97 That of Pikis J.

98 Judgment delivered by Triantafyllides P.

99 Judgment delivered by Triantafyllides P.

100 Article 11.6 reads: The judge before whom the person arrested is brought shall promptly proceed to inquire into the grounds of the arrest in a language understandable by the person arrested and shall, as soon as possible and in any event not later than three days from such appearance, either release the person arrested on such terms as he may deem fit or where the investigation into the commission of the offence for which he has been arrested has not been completed remand him in custody and may remand him in custody from time to time for a period not exceeding eight days at any one time. Provided that the total period of such remand in custody shall not exceed three months of the date of the arrest on the expiration of which every person or authority having the custody of the person arrested shall forthwith set him free. Any decision of the judge under this paragraph shall be subject to appeal.

prohibits the detention of a person for a purpose other than the one for which the individual is arrested. His detention for a purpose other than the one for which authorisation was sought and obtained sapped the warrant of its validity rendering the detention and whatever flowed therefrom illegal. The use of the investigation for purposes other than the ones for which detention was authorised derails the process and renders its offspring illegitimate (see *Aristotelous v. The Police (2002) 2 C.L.R. 225 (CA)*[101]).

In *Kattis a.o. v. Republic (2002) 2 C.L.R. 262 (CA) (majority judgment)*[102] the Court held that evidence deriving from a polluted source does constitute a violation of the principle of a fair trial. In arriving at this conclusion, the Court heeded and followed the ratio of the decision of the European Court of Human Rights in *Case of Teixeira de Castro v. Portugal, No. 44/1997/828/1034, 9th June 1998.* The principle acknowledged in the above decision was given effect to in *Psyllas v. Republic (2003) 2 C.L.R. 353 (CA)*[103].

8 In *Police v. Yiallourou (1992) 2 C.L.R. 147 (FB)*[104] the Supreme Court, giving expression to principles emerging from the case law, reiterated that a telephone conversation is an aspect of private life and an incident of freedom of communication protected respectively by Articles 15.1[106] and 17.1.[107] As a result, evidence deriving from the tapping of telephone communications of the accused was found to be inadmissible in criminal proceedings against one of the parties to the telephone conversation for abuse of office. The Court reminded that only limitations of human rights for a purpose permissible under the Constitution can legitimately restrict their application. The following passage from one of the judgments in *Georghiades* (supra)[105] puts the right to privacy and secrecy of communications in perspective:

> The rights guaranteed by Articles 15.1 and 17.1 fall in this category, aimed as they are, to safeguard the dignity of man and ensure a quality of life fit for man and his gifted nature.

---

[101] Judgment delivered by Pikis P.

[102] Majority judgment delivered by Pikis P., minority judgment delivered by Artemides J.

[103] Judgment delivered by Pikis P.

[104] Unanimous judgment, majority reasoning by Pikis J., separate reasoning by A. Loizou P. and Artemides J.

[105] That of Pikis J.

[106] It reads: Every person has the right to respect for his private and family life.

[107] It reads: Every person has the right to respect for, and to the secrecy of, his correspondence and other communication if such other communication is made through means not prohibited by law.

> The right to privacy is regarded as fundamental because of the protection it affords to the individuality of the person, on the one hand, and the space it offers for the development of his personality, on the other. Man is entitled to function autonomously in his private life and the right to privacy is aimed to shield him in this area from public gaze.

In *Georghiades* (supra) it was pointed out that privacy establishes the autonomy of man in private life and generates the proper climate for the development of the individual's personality releasing a person's creative (potential) faculties, so beneficial to the person and society as a whole. Intrusion into the private domain of man is not to be tolerated; without this guarantee, man's dignity and autonomy would be put to peril. To the submission that the search for truth overrides human rights the following answer was given in *Georghiades* (supra)[108]:

> The pursuit of truth is no warrant for watering down human rights. If that were allowed to happen fundamental rights would soon be chased out of the statute book. The recognition and effective enforcement of human rights is, in itself, an ultimate truth for the realisation of the human ideal, of supreme importance for the release of the creative forces in man. Recognition of human rights is a principal object of civilisation.

## III. Fundamental Principles of Justice

Article 12 incorporates fundamental norms of justice assured as the inalien- *9*
able rights of the individual. These principles formed, in the main, part of both the civil law and the English common law.

### 1. Nullum Crimen Sine Lege – Nulla Poena Sine Lege

Article 12.1 reads: *10*

> No person shall be held guilty of any offence on account of any act or omission which did not constitute an offence under the law at the time when it was committed; and no person shall have a heavier punishment imposed on him for an offence other than that expressly providing for it by law at the time when it was committed.

The criminalization of conduct is the domain of the law. An offence is distinguished from a moral shortfall or a sin.

---

[108] Judgment of Pikis J.

In *Republic v. Thalassinou (1991) 3 C.L.R. 203 (FB) (majority decision)* and *Vyronas v. Republic (1999) 3 C.L.R. 77 (FB) (majority decision)*, explained in greater detail in a subsequent chapter, the Supreme Court took the position that the principle embodied in Article 12(1) is all-embracive, extending even to conduct punishable under the Constitution. Thus, Article 150 of the Constitution conferring power upon the Supreme Constitutional Court and later the Supreme Court "to punish for contempt of itself" was held not to criminalize as such contemptuous conduct; for the reasons, on the one hand, that Article 150 did not specify the punishment to which the condemnor was liable and, on the other, that the statutory law did not cast it as an offence as such.

The principle enshrined in Article 12.1 that there shall be no conviction for conduct that is not criminalized by law is supplemented by the provision that punishment cannot be heavier than that provided by law at the time of the commission of the offence. Criminalization of conduct, generally, will not do. The maximum sentence to which the culprit is liable must be specified, acquainting thereby potential offenders of the punishment to which their conduct may expose them to.

In *Kophou a.o. v. The Police (1993) 2 C.L.R. 296 (CA)*[109] and *Philaktou v. The Police (1994) 2 C.L.R. 11 (CA)*[110] the Supreme Court remedied on appeal errors by the trial court resulting in the imposition of a sentence heavier than the one provided by law at the time of the commission of the criminal act. The sentence was reduced accordingly, adjusted within the parameters of the maximum sentence provided by law at the time the offence was committed.

2. The Rule Against Double Jeopardy

11 Article 12.2 reads:

> A person who has been acquitted or convicted of an offence shall not be tried again for the same offence. No person shall be punished twice for the same act or omission except where death ensues from such act or omission.

The principle entrenched in Article 12.2 found expression in Roman law under the maxim ne bis in idem and in the English common law by the rule against double jeopardy. The universality of the rule that a person shall not be

---

[109] Judgment delivered by Pikis J.
[110] Judgment delivered by Pikis J.

put in peril of conviction twice for the commission of the same offence (same criminal conduct) is qualified by the second part of Article 12.2 in the case of death resulting from a criminal act, the subject of punishment prior to the ensuance of death. The ensuing death adds a new dimension to the criminal conduct entailing a metamorphosis of the offence. An example may be provided by an assault committed with intent to cause grievous bodily harm to the victim, ultimately resulting in his/her death, whereupon the crime changes character and is classified as manslaughter. The correlation of death to criminal conduct is subject to the proviso set out in the Criminal Code (Section 213) that death must result within a year and a day.

The case of *Pernell a.o. v. Republic (No. 1) (1998) 2 C.L.R. 177 (CA)*[111] illustrates the strictness of the rule against double jeopardy. Upon the appeal of the accused against their conviction on a count of homicide, the respondent, the prosecuting authority, sought to adduce evidence that emerged or was collected after the trial in support of the conviction. An appeal under the Cyprus system of justice as in England is primarily confined to a review of the correctness of the judgment of the trial court. The Supreme Court rejected the application of the Attorney General for the reason that admission of such evidence would violate the provisions of Article 12.2. Admitting such evidence would be tantamount to acknowledging a second opportunity to the prosecution to prove its case, putting the accused in peril of conviction twice. A similar issue was likewise determined in *Christodoulou alias Ropas a.o. v. Republic (No. 1) (2000) 2 C.L.R. 294 (CA)*.[112] In *Attorney-General v. Vassiliou (2003) 2 C.L.R. 21 (CA)*[113] a different question arose involving the punishment of the accused twice for the same offence. Upon the conviction of the accused for drug offences and ponderation of the sentence to be imposed, the trial court concluded that a sentence of imprisonment was merited. Sequentially, the court judged it appropriate in face of the circumstances of the case and those of the accused to suspend the sentence. Thereafter, the court imposed a heavy monetary penalty on the accused seemingly because the sentence of imprisonment was suspended. It is settled under Cyprus law that suspension of a sentence does not change the character of imprisonment as a punitive measure. Failing compliance with the conditions of suspension, a sentence of imprisonment

[111] Judgment delivered by Pikis P.
[112] Judgment delivered by Pikis P.
[113] Judgment delivered by Pikis P.

may be activated. The Supreme Court held that the imposition of the fine was tantamount to punishing the accused twice for the same offence.

The application of the principle enshrined in Article 12.2 is not limited to criminal proceedings. It extends as acknowledged in *Philippou v. Disciplinary Council (2000) 1 C.L.R. 1839 (CA)*[114] to disciplinary proceedings too and to any proceedings, it would seem, where a person is accused of having done something contrary to rule or regulation. Of course, the same conduct may constitute a criminal as well as a disciplinary offence. In that case, as explained at a subsequent stage, there is no prohibition in pursuing both proceedings. In disciplinary proceedings, the rule against double jeopardy takes the form of not exposing the accused to the peril of conviction for the same disciplinary offence twice. In the above case, the advocates' disciplinary council suspended the licence of a lawyer who had been adjudged bankrupt. Subsequently, the disciplinary council decided to extend the suspension until the end of bankruptcy and the reinstatement of the bankrupt. The Court discharged the extension of the disqualification holding that it amounted to a second punishment of the accused for the same disciplinary offence.

### 3. Punishment – The Sole Province of the Judiciary

*12* Article 12.3 reads:

> No law shall provide for a punishment which is disproportionate to the gravity of the offence.

The punishment of crime is the exclusive territory of the Judiciary. Consequently, pre-independence legislation prescribing a minimum sentence for the commission of a crime was repeatedly found to be incompatible with Article 12.3.[115] Judicial discretion with regard to the form of punishment for the commission of an offence or the measure of it cannot be fettered by any of the other powers of the State. Article 7.2 makes an exception to this rule. It provides that the death penalty may be prescribed by law

[114] Judgment delivered by Pikis P.

[115] see inter alia The District Officer, Nicosia and Georghios Haji Yiannis 1 R.S.C.C. 79, The District Officer, Famagusta and Dem. Panayiotou Antoni 1 R.S.C.C. 84, The Superintendent Gendarmerie Lefka and Christodoulos A. Hadji Yianni 2 R.S.C.C. 21, Morphu Gendarmerie and Andreas Demetri Englezos 3 R.S.C.C. 7, The District Officer, The Nicosia and Miachael Ktori Palis 3 R.S.C.C. 27, The District Officer Famagusta and Michael Themistocli a.o. 3 R.S.C.C. 47, Nicosia Police and Djemal Ahmed 3 R.S.C.C. 50, The District Officer, Kyrenia and Adem Salih 3 R.S.C.C. 69, Miliotis v. The Police (1975) 7 J.S.C. 933.

for the following offences: premeditated murder, high treason, piracy jure gentium and capital offences under military law. Under the Criminal Code premeditated murder carried the death penalty. This ceased to be the case in 1983 by an amendment of the law (L-86/83) substituting life imprisonment for the death penalty.

Prescription of the maximum sentence, on the other hand, is not only permissible but required by Article 12.1 as a necessary attribute of a criminal offence. Both, the definition and the penal categorization of a crime are in the power of the Legislature.

In determining the gravity of an offence objective and subjective considerations enter the equation. The first relate to the seriousness of the offence from the societal point of view and the second to the person of the accused, his/her understanding, circumstances and motives for the commission of the offence. A destitute person stealing a loaf of bread is in a different position from another person stealing the same to enrich himself/herself. The individualization of a sentence so as to fit not only the offence but also the person of the offender is an axiom of penal justice reflected in many decided cases.[116] It has often been said that the higher one stands the greater is his/her responsibility to abide by the law. The circumstances of a person may mitigate as well as aggravate the seriousness of the offence. Such was found to be the case in *Pengeros v. Republic (1995) 2 C.L.R. 143 (CA)*[117] where a member of the police was found guilty of possessing explosive substances. In *Demetriou v. Republic (1984) 2 C.L.R. 323 (CA)*[118] the diminished responsibility of the accused on account of mental illness was treated as a factor mitigating the gravity of the offence.

Another principle of criminal justice is parity of treatment. Offenders who are in a similar position must be likewise treated. The approach to parity of treatment of offenders is reflected in the following passage from the judgment of the Court in *Koukos v. The Police (1986) 1 C.L.R. 1 (CA)*[119]: *13*

> Parity of treatment of persons in substantially the same position is a deep rooted principle of criminal justice, interwoven with the wider ends of justice. Equality before the law and the administration of justice is constitutionally safeguarded in Cyprus by the provisions of Article 28.1 of the Constitution.

[116] Riley v. The Police (1989) 2 C.L.R. 335.
[117] Judgment delivered by Pikis P.
[118] Judgment delivered by Pikis J.
[119] Judgment delivered by Pikis P.

> Disparity of sentences is, as proclaimed in *Nicolaou v. The Police [(1969) 2 C.L.R. 120]*, offensive to common sense and derogatory of equality before the law. In this, as in other respects, equality does not connote mathematical nicety; nor is the principle of parity of sentences designed to blunt the sentencing process by eliminating the discretion of the trial Court to impose on each of the accused a sentence that takes due account of both the intrinsic culpability of his conduct and personal circumstances. For disparity to make an impact on appeal the difference between the sentences imposed must be substantial, such as to suggest, in the face of strong similarity in the position of the accused, that justice is not done and for that reason liable to generate feelings of injustice on the part of the appellant. Unjustified differences in the treatment of persons jointly accused tend to undermine faith in the law and the administration of justice.[120]

The case law establishes that the treatment of offenders for purposes of equality is not confined to the punishment meted out by the Court but extends to the treatment of offenders by the prosecuting authority. Under Article 113.2 the Attorney General is empowered to discontinue criminal proceedings by entering a nolle prosecqui. It has been held time and again that such action is relevant to the treatment of a co-accused justifying a reduction of the sentence that might otherwise be imposed on the latter assuaging in that way the sense of injustice generated by unequal treatment. (See *Demetriou* (supra), *Kattou a.o. v. The Police (1991) 2 C.L.R. 498 (CA) (majority decision)*,[121] *Ioannou v. The Police (No.2) (1997) 2 C.L.R. 267 (P) (majority decision)*[122]). This is not a very nice (precise) way to remedy the ill-effects of inequality, but it is the only means available to the Court. A question that has attracted conflicting decisions is whether the presidential prerogative to remit, suspend or commute a sentence (Article 53.4) has a bearing on the parity of treatment of offenders. In *Kafkaros a.o. v. Republic (1995) 2 C.L.R. 5 (CA)*,[123] pending the hearing of an appeal against conviction and sentence by persons convicted and sentenced for the same offence, the sentence of one of them was remitted by the President of the Republic. The Supreme Court took the view that this was a consideration relevant to equality of treatment, a fact duly reflected in the sentences imposed on the

[120] The passage stems from page 16 of the judgment. Article 28.1. provides: "All persons are equal before the law, the administration and justice and are entitled to equal protection thereof and treatment thereby."

[121] Majority judgments delivered by Artemides J., Nicolaou J., Kallis J., Elidiades J.; minority judgment delivered by Pikis P.

[122] Majority judgment delivered by Pikis P; minority judgment delivered by Nicolaou J.

[123] Judgment delivered by Pikis P.

others. This decision was not followed in *Ioannou v. The Police (supra)* as the exercise of the privilege of the President is not in any way subject to review.[124] The minority held otherwise. In their opinion the non-reviewability of the decision of the President is not a decisive factor as it is not a decisive factor in the case of the discontinuance of proceedings by the Attorney-General.

Previous convictions and especially a burdened criminal record are an aggravating factor and provide grounds for differentiation with respect to the punishment meted out to the co-accused, both in the choice of punishment and the length of it. However, as stressed in *Ioannou v. The Police (1989) 2 C.L.R. 251 (CA)*,[125] the differentiation must not be disproportionate to the significance of this factor in the sentencing process.

### 4. The Presumption of Innocence – The Right Against Self-Crimination

Article 12.4 *14*

> Every person charged with an offence shall be presumed innocent until proved guilty according to law.

The presumption of innocence is deeply rooted in both legal systems developed in Europe. This is perhaps the most significant component of the liberty of man. Suspicion has no sway. Only in the face of proof of guilt beyond reasonable doubt is the presumption displaced.

In *President of the Republic v. House of Representatives (No. 1) (1994) 3 C.L.R. 1 (P)*[126] the Court pronounced that the presumption of innocence imports the right to silence and sequentially thereto the right against self-crimination. Consequently, the Registration of Unlicensed Apartments Law (1981) was declared unconstitutional inasmuch as it imposed an obligation upon the owners of such establishments to declare the fact that they were operating unlicensed apartments to the authorities. Such declaration necessarily entailed disclosure of criminal conduct, it being an offence to use unlicensed premises as hotel apartments. The right to silence is in the words of the Court in an earlier case absolute; it admits of no qualifications. No adverse inferences can be drawn from its exercise *(Charalambous v. Republic (1985) 2 C.L.R. 97 (CA)*[127]*)*.

---

[124] Ioannou v. The Police (No. 1) (1997) 2 C.L.R. 147.

[125] Judgment delivered by Pikis J.

[126] Judgment delivered by A. Loizou P.

[127] Judgment delivered by Pikis J.

In *Case of John Murray v. The United Kingdom Application No. 18731/91, 8th February 1996,* the European Court of Human Rights underlined the close connection between the right to silence and the right against self-crimination without directly acknowledging the latter as being an offspring of the former. In its subsequent decision in *Case of Allan v. The United Kingdom Application No. 48539/99, 5th November 2002,* the European Court of Human Rights underlined, "The right not to incriminate oneself is primarily concerned with respecting the will of the person to remain silent".

In *Psyllas v. Republic (2003) 2 C.L.R. 353 (CA)*[128] the accused, while in police custody, refused to provide genetic material at the request of the police deemed necessary for the investigation of the crimes for which he was detained. To circumvent his objections, the police offered him refreshment in a bottle provided with a straw wherefrom they elicited his DNA. Such evidence was subsequently used at his trial on charges of burglary and house-breaking leading to his conviction. The Supreme Court set aside the conviction and acquitted the accused on the ground that the evidence was collected in breach of his right against self-crimination. It is of interest to note the remarks of the Court that any attempt on the part of the police to extract from the suspect genetic material by force would violate the provisions of Article 7.1. guaranteeing the bodily integrity of the individual.

The above decision was not followed in the subsequent case of *Republic v. Avramidou a.o. (2004) 2 C.L.R. 51 (P) (majority decision)*[129]. At issue was the admissibility of DNA traced in the stump of a cigarette smoked by the accused obtained by the police by surreptitious means in order to bypass his refusal to provide genetic material. The majority adjudged that the rule against self-crimination is limited to verbal statements deriving in this respect support from dicta in the decision of the European Court of Human Rigths (see *Case of Saunders v. The United Kingdom Application No. 19187/91, 17th December 1996 and Case of Heaney and Mc Guiness v. Republic of Ireland, Application No. 34720/97, 21st December 2000*). Consequently, the principle against self-crimination was held to be inapplicable where evidence stemmed from the body of the accused as opposed to vocal expressions from the same person. Hence, the rule against self-crimination applies to oral in contrast to real evidence. The minority adhered to the ratio in *Psyllas* (supra) holding that the evidence in question had been secured in breach of the principle

---

[128] Judgment delivered by Pikis P.

[129] Majority judgments by Artemides J., Gavrielides J. and Hadjihambis J.; minority judgments by Pikis P. and Kallis J.

against self-crimination but also in contravention of the rule requiring the exclusion of evidence deriving from a polluted source. Furthermore, they held that the evidence was objectionable for breach of the conditions of detention of the suspect not authorized for the purpose of extracting evidence from his person while in custody. As indicated in one of the minority judgments, it is difficult to sustain the dichotomy between the mind and the body of a person for evidential purposes. In either case, the material consideration is the will of the individual; whether he/she voluntarily abandoned the right to silence. A human being is an indivisible entity at all times, the hallmark of his/her persona in law and in every other respect.

## IV. Human Rights Foreshadow the System of Government

Human rights define the rights of man as a physical and social entity. *15*
Assurance of the status of man in society defines in large measure the system of government, the framework and parameters of the law, as it was pointed out in *President of the Republic v. House of Representatives (2000) 3 C.L.R. 238 (P).*[130]

A system of representative democracy is foreshadowed by the right to vote in every election to be held at predetermined intervals of time. The right to equality before the law, under the law and equal protection thereof and treatment thereby requires assurance of isonomy, isopolity and isocracy that binds the State to legislate and act in all spheres of action in a corresponding manner. Respect for privacy and family life makes the private domain of a person invulnerable to intrusion by state authorities or anybody else. Freedom of thought, conscience and speech, the emblems of freedom of man, define the social context within which man can function fruitfully. The right to social security binds society to protect the individual from want. On the other hand, the duty to contribute to public burdens according to one's means is meant to shield the individual from want that afflicts the dignity of man. The right to education provides the ground for the intellectual ascent of man. The rights to life, bodily integrity and freedom of movement assure a meaningful existence binding society to shield human beings from foreseeable dangers to life and body. The guarantee of justice for man may be acclaimed as the nucleus of an anthropocentric society.

---

[130] Judgment delivered by Pikis P.

16 In *President of the Republic v. House of Representatives (2000)* (supra) the Court was required to determine whether a law obliging high State officials to submit details of their property and that of family members infringed the right to privacy established by Article 15.1. Both parties acknowledged and the Court affirmed that the financial affairs of a person are a part of private life. Paragraph 2 of Article 15 permits a limitation to the right of privacy and family life:

> only in the interests of the security of the Republic or the constitutional order or the public safety or the public order or the public health or the public morals or for the protection of the rights and liberties guaranteed by this Constitution to any person.

In the absence of indication that anyone of the purposes for which the right to privacy could be limited was in danger or at risk, the limitations imposed could not but be deemed to be in breach of the Constitution; as indeed the law in question was pronounced to be. Before a human right may justifiably be limited or restricted, it must be demonstrated, as the Court noted, that one or more of the causes for which limitation is permissible is in real danger to an extent making necessary the limitation in order to avert it. For a perceived danger to a constitutional goal for the protection of which limitation of a human right is permissible, it must be made to appear that the emergence of it is imminent creating a pressing need to forestall it. To this, the following rider must be added: The limitation imposed must not be greater than absolutely necessary to prevent the manifestation of the danger. The Court reiterated that the final arbiters of the existence of the danger and the justification of the measures to avert it are the courts of law. The existence of a threat to a given constitutional cause is not presumed by the mere fact that the Legislature seeks to take measures to protect it. The perceived danger must be specified in the preamble to the law as well as the reasons founding it. Even then the recitation of the relevant facts in the preamble is not conclusive; the Court must be satisfied that the danger does exist and the need to prevent it by the limitation of a human right pressing. Short of that, any attempt to limit a human right is doomed to failure. In evaluating the existence of a danger, judicial notice may be taken of facts constituting common knowledge.

The following propositions emerge from the judgment of the Court in *President of the Republic v. The House of Representatives (2000)* above:

a) Human rights are attuned to human nature; the defining element of their configuration.

b) Blood or family relationship provides no ground for interference with the privacy of another person.
c) In their private life individuals are autonomous.

Another decision illuminating the scene with regard to the prerequisites for the limitation of human rights is *Georghiou a.o. v. The Police (1999) 2 C.L.R. 616 (CA)*[131]. The case concerned the constitutionality of a law prescribing a second afternoon off for shop assistants (Wednesday in addition to Saturday afternoon). Article 25.1 guarantees the right to practise any profession or to carry on any occupation, trade or business subject to such formalities, conditions or restrictions imposed in the public interest. The Court concluded that the limitation was justified in the public interest by the amenity it allowed to employees to engage in activities associated with family and personal life, in harmony with human nature; on the other hand the limitation was not such as to strike at the nucleus of the right of the freedom to trade.

## V. Limitation of Human Rights

Before embarking upon a discussion of possible limitations to human rights, *17*
we must define the ambit of the rights assured to man. The boundaries of human rights are delineated by reference to the corresponding right of every other person. The fundamental rights of one person must correspond to the same rights of the next person. The rights of one man must be enjoyed and exercised in harmony with those of every other human being. Ensuring the parallel enjoyment and exercise of human rights by every person does not involve their limitation but the identification of their inherent remit. Respect for the rights of others is a sine qua non for the assurance of human rights. Giving legislative expression to the discharge of this duty, respect for the rights of others does not involve derogation from human rights. On the contrary, violation of the rights of others may attract penal sanctions and/or civil law consequences.

Not all rights guaranteed in Part II of the Constitution admit of restrictions *18*
or limitations. A notable example is Article 28 entrenching equality in all respects, guaranteeing isonomy, isocracy, isopolity. Equality admits of no limitation as the decision in *Republic v. Constantinou (2002) 3 C.L.R. 534*

---

131 Majority judgment delivered by Pikis P., minority judgment delivered by Hadjihambis J.

*(FB) (majority decision)*[132] acknowledges.[133] Dissimilar treatment can only be justified by dissimilarities between the subjects of the law such as would cast them in heterogeneous categories. The test for identifying similarities or dissimilarities hinges on the object and purpose of the law by reference to which they are introduced.

*19* Limitations or restrictions of human rights are by definition temporary measures coextensive in duration with the necessity that warranted their imposition. Limitations outlasting the necessity that led to their adoption can find no justification. At the end or eclipse of the necessity that warranted the limitation of a human right it is the duty of the Legislature to abrogate the limitative enactment. Failure to do so does not, it appears, absolve the Judiciary of the duty to inquire into the subsistence of the necessity and, if it ceased to exist, to disclaim the limitative measures. In *President of the Republic v. House of Representatives (2000)* (supra) the Court indicated that the Legislature is duty bound to repeal a law limitative of human rights when the necessity that led to its introduction ceases to exist or disappears. Provided need arises to limit the application of a human right, the limitation must be coextensive with the danger posed to a given constitutional objective and go no further. In other words, the limitative measures must be strictly proportionate to the need to safeguard the specified constitutional objective in the interest of which they are imposed.

Unlike human rights the inalienability of which is assured by the Constitution, rights conferred by ordinary law may be subjected to conditions or limitations at the discretion of the Legislature. In *Antoniou v. The Police (1989) 2 C.L.R. 299 (CA)*[134] the Court was invited to reject a traffic regulation requiring the wearing of a safety belt while driving as unconstitutional on the ground that it interfered with the right of freedom of movement safeguarded by Article 13.[135] The Court rejected the plea explaining

---

[132] Majority decision by Pikis P., concurring separate decision by Artemides J.; minority decision by Nicolaides J.

[133] The facts of the case are given on page 130.

[134] Judgment delivered by Pikis J.

[135] It reads: 1. Every person has the right to move freely throughout the territory of the Republic and to reside in any part thereof subject to any restrictions imposed by law and which are necessary only for the purposes of defence or public health or provided as punishment to be passed by a competent court.

2. Every person has the right to leave permanently or temporarily the territory of the Republic subject to reasonable restrictions imposed by law.

that the right to drive, to which the duty to wear a safety belt is attached, is not a right deriving from the nature of man but a right given by law and as such, subject to terms and conditions deemed necessary for its exercise. A different answer was given to the acceptability of a restriction for the use of lawful means adapted for the transportation of persons, notably cars, prohibiting their use on alternate week-ends, depending on the number on their plates. The measure was taken in order to reduce petrol consumption. The Court pronounced the limitation to be unconstitutional in *Elia v. Republic (1980) 2 C.L.R. 118 (CA)*[136] for the reason that it limited freedom of movement by lawful means throughout the Republic guaranteed by Article 13. The ratio of the case is that freedom of movement confers an unfettered right to use every lawful means to move about the country. The measure entailed limitation of the use of a car and not the prescription of the conditions for its use.

## VI. Imposition of a Duty to Exercise Human Rights

The jurisprudence of the Supreme Court accepts that there is no impedi- *20*
ment to coupling a right with a duty to exercise it. In *Pingouras v. Police (1987) 2 C.L.R. 1 (CA)*[137] the Court held that making the exercise of the right to vote in elections compulsory was not unconstitutional. It did not infringe Article 31 guaranteeing to every citizen the right to vote in any election held under the Constitution or any law. The Constitution provides for presidential and parliamentary elections within fixed intervals of time and by-elections to fill vacancies occurring in between. The Court emphasized that the duty imposed to exercise the right to vote was interwoven with the essence of the right, namely to assure the participation of a person in the common affairs, intended to ensure that government derives from the people. The right to participate in public affairs and the responsibility for the choice of the ruling body is historically linked to the genesis of democracy in Ancient Greece. If people abstained from participating in the election of government, the right would be defeated and its object frustrated. Another example of a duty being imposed to exercise a human right relates to Articles 12.5 and Article 30. 2 and 3; in particular one's right to be present at one's

[136] Judgment delivered by Triantafyllides P.

[137] Judgments delivered by A. Loizou J. and Pikis J.

trial. Section 44 (1) of the Criminal Procedural Law CAP 155, imposes a duty upon the accused to be present at his/her trial for a serious offence. In *Republic v. Demetriades a.o. (1973) 2 C.L.R. 289 (FB) (majority judgment)*,[138] the Supreme Court held that the duty imposed upon the accused by the Criminal Procedure Law to be present at his trial in a serious criminal case (Section 63(3)) is not contradictory to his right to be present, assured by Article 6 (3) of the European Convention. The Court noted that the imposition of the duty is not exogenous to the purpose for which the right to be present is assured.

The underlying principle is that a duty imposed to exercise a human right involves no antithesis to the freedom to exercise the right so long as the reasons for imposing it are associated with the ends that the human right is intended to serve and uphold. Arguably, the answer would be different if the duty was imposed for a purpose unconnected with the efficacy of the right.

## VII. Access to the Court

*21* Unimpeded access to the Court for the assertion or vindication of one's rights is acknowledged by Article 30.1 as a fundamental right of the individual. Article 158 envisages the establishment by law of courts subordinate to the superior court in sufficient numbers for the undelayed administration of justice and the efficient application of human rights. The Courts of Justice Law 1960 (L-14/60), enacted soon after independence, makes provision for the establishment within the framework of the judicial power of District Courts and Assize Courts with jurisdiction, competencies and powers analogous to those of corresponding bodies founded during colonial rule; a judicial structure corresponding to the prototype of courts established in colonies of the British Crown. In time, need arose to transfer aspects of the jurisdiction of the District Courts to coordinate first instance courts. The distinctiveness of the jurisdiction trusted to such courts was the reason for its assignment to separate courts. In consequence, the following courts with specialized jurisdiction were established: a) a Military Court set up by the Military Code and Criminal Procedure Law of 1964, (L-40/64) b) the Industrial Disputes Court provided for by law L-8/67 c) the Rent Control

[138] The majority judgment was given by Triantafyllides P. – the minority judgment was delivered by Hadjianastassiou J.

Court founded by law L-23/83 and d) the Family Court introduced by law L-23/90.

A constitutional issue that attracted the attention of the Court on a number of occasions was whether prescription of periods of limitation for the exercise of a right accruing under the law are reconcilable with freedom of access to the court safeguarded by Article 30.1. The answer to the question, as it emerges from the case law, may be summed up in the following proposition: The limitation of the time within which an entrenched right may be exercised is permissible so long as it is not restrictive to the point of violating the nucleus of the right. Freedom of access to the court assures amenity to ponder over one's rights and reflect upon them and latitude to prepare for their assertion. The first case of the kind that came before the Court affected the legitimacy of a three month period of limitation for raising an action against the Electricity Authority, a public corporation, for wrongful action in the exercise of its powers. The period of limitation was declared to be incompatible with the freedom of access to the court assured to a person by Article 30.1 as well as the right to equality inasmuch as victims of similar tortious conduct in other areas had a wider margin to pursue their rights (see *Fekkas v. The Electricity Authority of Cyprus (1967) 1 C.L.R. 173 (CA)*[139]). 22

In *Georgallas v. Hadjichristodoulou (2000) 1 C.L.R. 2060 (FB)*[140] the Court was asked to pronounce on the constitutionality of Section 11(1)(a) of the Children Relationship and Legal Status Law 1991 (L-187/91) providing that paternity could be disclaimed within one year from birth or from the date of receiving knowledge of the crucial facts relevant to paternity. The Court found the period of one year reasonable since it left the quintessence of the right unaffected, affording to the presumed father reasonable freedom to disown paternity. Access to the court and periods of limitations are, it must be noted, correlated to the rights of others and to certainty in relation to their rights and legal status. The Court underlined that the need for certainty about a person's rights and determination of disputes within a reasonable time are fundamental for the fruitful enjoyment of one's rights and the timely discharge of obligations. Decisions of the European Court of Human Rights and the European Commission on Human Rights acknowledge the legitimacy of periods of prescription so long as the period is reasonable having regard to

[139] Judgment delivered by Triantafyllides J.
[140] Judgment delivered by Pikis P.

the nature of the right.[141] The equitable principle of "laches" under English law to which reference is also made in the aforesaid judgment of the Supreme Court, recognises that inordinate delay in the exercise of a right, accompanied by circumstances that render its pursuit unjust raise a barrier to a claim founded upon it. In *Karadjias v. Papakyriakou (2001) 1 C.L.R. 2113 (FB)*[142] the Court held that a prescriptive period of two years envisaged by Section 14 of law L-232/91 for raising claims against the former spouse after the dissolution or annulment of marriage did not infringe Article 30.1. In *Finikaridou v. Odysseos (2001) 1 C.L.R. 1744 (FB) (majority decision)*[143] the Court was divided in answering the question whether the prescription of the right of a child to seek recognition of paternity three years after attaining majority violated the provision of Article 30.1. The three year period was set independently of knowledge on the part of the child of the facts relevant to paternity. The majority held that the period of limitation was reasonable allowing a fair margin for the ascertainment of facts relevant to one's paternity and as such not contradictory to Article 30.1. The petitioner in the case before the Court gained knowledge about who his father was from his mother many years after attaining majority, just before her death. The minority concluded that the disassociation of the prescriptive period from knowledge of the facts relevant to the accrual of the right made access to the Court impossible. In their view, the accrual of a right cannot be divorced from possible knowledge about its existence, a prerequisite for its assertion. Prescription of a right at a time when the beneficiary can have no knowledge of it defies the right of access to the Court to proclaim it. Access to the court is assured for the vindication of a right. Article 30.1 does not of itself confer a right of action where none exists. Thus, a term in an insurance contract that an action for damages raised within a specified period of time from the dismissal of a claim to compensation by the insurers was found to be non-offensive to Article 30.1 in *Pittara v. Cosmos (Insurance) Co. Ltd. (1998) 1 C.L.R. 193 (CA)*.[144] The Court held that the relevant term was part of the contract of the parties, freely agreed upon, definitive of the accrual of a right to pursue an action for damages

---

[141] See inter alia: Case of Stubbings a.o. v. The United Kingdom Application No. 22083/93, 22095/93, 22nd October 1996.

[142] Judgment delivered by Pikis P.

[143] The majority judgment was delivered by Artemides J, the minority judgment delivered by Pikis P.

[144] Judgment delivered by Pikis P.

before the court. Freedom of contract is assured as a fundamental right by Article 26.1. As clarified in *President of the Republic v. House of Representatives (1997) 3 C.L.R. 36 (P)*,[145] freedom of contract includes both the formation of the contract and the content of its terms.

## VIII. Essence of Human Rights

23 Human nature is the definitive element for the ascertainment of the content and compass of human rights. Aristotle identified man as a political animal. The entwined nature of man, a person's physiology and predisposition to political life define his/her rights. In *Yiallouros v. Nicolaou (2001) 1 C.L.R 558 (FB)*[146] the Court in awarding damages for intrusion into the plaintiff's privacy stressed that the object of the exercise is to afford such relief to the person as may justly compensate a human being as a physical and social entity. Due appreciation of the nature of man is essential both for the definition and the scope of his/her rights and the relief necessary to assuage injury thereto. Human rights are perceived as inborn, an incident of human nature, inhering in man as an attribute of human identity.

In *Community of Pyrga a.o. v. Republic a.o. (1991) 4 C.L.R. 3498 (SJ)*[147] the Court was required to explore the breadth of the right to life guaranteed by Article 7.1. The question raised was whether the right to life confers upon the community and its members a say in the environment in which they live. At issue was the legitimacy of the right of the applicants to seek review of a decision of the Administration authorizing the sinking of a quarry on the outskirts of their village. The Court decided that the right to life legitimises persons likely to be affected by the quarry's operation to seek judicial review of a decision to license it. The Court took pains to stress that the Constitution is no ordinary law but the founding law of the State. The principles and values embodied therein, in relation to human rights, are timeless, referable to the nature of man not the time of his/her life.

Accepting, as the Court did, the legitimacy of the interest of the applicants, it issued an order suspending the operation of the quarry pending trial; upon review the decision was annulled. On appeal the outcome was

145 Judgment delivered by Pikis P.

146 Majority reasoning delivered by Pikis P., concurring reasoning delivered by Artemides J.

147 Judgment delivered by Pikis J.

confirmed save that the Court refrained from expressing a conclusive view on the implications of the right to life on the environment (see *The Republic v. Community of Pyrga (1991) 4 C.L.R. 3498 (FB)*[148]).

As the case law establishes, constitutional provisions should be interpreted from a diachronic perspective, more so provisions incorporating human rights. In *Attorney-General v. Georghiou (1984) 2 C.L.R. 251 (FB) (majority decision)*[149] the Court pointed out that the Constitution is no ordinary statute but the basic source of law cast in a separate category, not subject to the ordinary rules of interpretation (see also *Georghiades* (supra) and *President of the Republic v. House of Representatives (No. 2) (2001) 3 C.L.R. 519 (P)*[150]). Human rights entrenched therein embody fundamental norms to be given effect to in the ever changing social context. As stated in *Yangou 'Lemonas' v. The Police (2001) 2 C.L.R. 421 (CA)*[151] "The provisions of the Constitution including those of paragraph c of Article 12.5 must be applied with the breadth befitting constitutional provisions safeguarding human rights." Human rights have a transcendental character to be upheld in the fluctuating social circumstances at all times. Man is the cell of society; society should evolve around the person not above it or independently of the individual.

24 A matter of importance is whether human rights can be waived or relinquished by their vestee, the person. The answer to the question cannot be extricated from the nature of human rights. In *Cleanthous a.o. v. Cyprus Telecommunication Authority (1991) 4 C.L.R. 297 (SJ)*[152] it was decided that there is no room for the compromise or relinquishment of human rights by the vestee or anybody else. The obligation cast upon the authorities of the State by Article 35 to ensure the effective application of human rights is consonant with the treatment of human rights as inalienable. Can one agree to be struck? Can one agree to be humiliated? These rhetorical questions admit of one answer only, no. The very idea of waiving one's fundamental rights suggests amenity to disown one's being or degrade one's self. Human rights originate from the nature of an indivisible being, whose physical integrity, dignity and identity are inseparable elements of the same

148 Majority judgments delivered by Artemides J., and Chrysostomis J. minority judgment delivered by Nikitas J.

149 Majority judgments delivered by Pikis J., Hadjianastassiou J., A. Loizou J., Malachtos J.; minority judgment delivered by Triantafyllides P., Loris J. and Stylianides J.

150 Judgment delivered by Pikis P.

151 Judgment delivered by Pikis P.

152 Judgment delivered by Pikis J.

entity. Article 34 stipulates that no acts should be suffered leading to the destruction of the guaranteed rights and liberties of the individual.

Human rights define the identity of individuals and their status. There is no 25
hierarchy of human rights. They have a common origin in human existence and a common purpose, its sustenance. The Greek term for human rights "atomika dikeomata" ("atomic" rights) depicts them as part of the nucleus of human existence. And inasmuch as an atom is perceived as an indivisible particle[153] so are the rights of men indivisible. The essence of human rights in the social context is encapsulated in the following proposition: *the good of the multitude is inseverable from the good of the individual.*

The proposition that human rights cannot be waived by a person was not accepted by the majority of the Supreme Court in *Doros Georghiades – Civil Appeal 11355 (3 October 2002) (FB).*[154] At issue was the amenity of the accused in a criminal trial to waive his right to a public hearing in relation to part of the proceedings. Another issue in the case was whether habeas corpus could be invoked to impugn a conviction as a substitute for an appeal. That this is not possible met with the unanimous approval of the Court; a fact that sealed the outcome of the proceedings. The disagreement affected amenity to waive a human right, trial in public. Because of their nature, charges for sexual offences, the accused agreed that part of the proceedings being held in camera. The majority concluded, in line with decisions of the European Court of Human Rights on the subject,[155] that a person may waive a right, in this case the right to a public hearing. The minority was led to a different conclusion in view of the nature of human rights and the imperative provisions of Article 35 casting a duty on every power of the State to ensure their effective application. What remains uncertain after the judgment of the Court is whether every human right can be waived or only those rights waiver of which does not antagonize the purpose they are designed to serve, in that case a fair trial; in essence procedural safeguards.

---

153 That is what the word atom means; nowadays science perceives the atom as having subparts electron and proton.

154 Not yet reported, majority judgment delivered by Kallis J, minority judgment delivered by Pikis P.

155 See Case of Albert and Le Compte v. Belgium Application No. 2689/65, 17th January 1970; Case of Hakansson and Sturesson v. Sweden Application No. 11855/85, 21st February 1990; see also: Case of Poitrimol v. France Application No. 14032/88, 23rd November 1993 (waiver of the right to be present at the hearing); Case of Deweer v. Belgium Application No. 6903/75, 27th February 1980 (waiver to the right to access to the court).

## IX. Remedies for Breach of Human Rights

26 In *Georghiades* (supra), there are dicta to the effect that breach of the fundamental rights of a person, be it by the State or a fellow human being, bestows upon the injured party an actionable right to invoke constitutional and municipal law remedies for the recovery of damage or other relief. The above dicta were adopted as part of the ratio of the judgment of the Court in *Yiallourou* (supra). The plaintiff raised an action for damages against the defendant for breach of his right to privacy occasioned by intrusion into his telephone conversations. The plaintiff had suffered no financial loss. The trial court awarded him 5.000 Cyprus Pounds damages (equivalent to about 9.000 EUR). The defendant disputed the award of damages in an appeal lodged against the trial court's decision. He argued that breach of human rights is not actionable per se. Only if the breach of human rights involves conduct constituting a civil wrong, it is actionable. The Court decided that the duty to protect human rights requires the availability of redress as a necessary means for sustaining their efficacy. Furthermore, Article 13 of the European Convention envisages the availability of an effective remedy before the national courts to a person whose freedoms and liberties are violated. The Court examined at length the measure of damages appropriate for the compensation of a victim of violation of human rights. Extensive reference was made to the principle of English law underlying compensation to a wronged party namely restitutio ab integrum and the principle of moral damage applicable in continental law. The Court indicated that the principles of the two systems of law in relation to compensation of an injured party largely converge. Just compensation lies at the root of both systems. The injury inflicted by breach of a person's human rights is ascertained by reference to the wrong done to man as a physical and as a social entity. Agony, humiliation, psychological trauma, the degradation inherent therewith and injury to one's well-being are all factors to be taken into account in determining the compensation payable.

27 It is worth noting that in the English case of *Anufrijeva a.o. v. Southwark London BC (2004) 1 All E.R. 833* the Court of Appeal held that breach of human rights does not entitle the victim per se to compensation. A case of compensation may arise if the breach is accompanied by an element of culpability, indicative of lack of respect for the right in question. In the particular case the right breached was that of private and family life. Damages it was said "were not recoverable as of right in the case of a claim brought

under the 1998 Act for breach of the convention". The Court construed the case law of the European Court of Human Rights as supporting the position they espoused. They relied mostly on the fact that on many occasions the European Court of Human Rights confined redress to acknowledgement of breach of the right without an accompanying order for compensation. A subsequent decision *R (Greenfield) v. Sec. of State (2005) 2 All E.R. 240 (HL)* suggests that in the absence of special features associated with the violation of human rights mere acknowledgment of the breach would accord due satisfaction. Thus, the claim of a prisoner, whose right under Article 6.1 of the European Convention on Human Rights for an impartial and independent tribunal had been violated by an adjudication made by the Deputy Controller of a privately managed prison holding him liable for the commission of drug offences, was deemed to be satisfied by a declaration that his Article 6.1 right had been breached; refusing his claim to compensation.

The distinction between acts classified as civil wrongs and acts constituting breaches of human rights in terms of actionability and compensation cannot find justification. In either case we are confronted with a violation of the rights of a person. The law of tort was developed prior to the recognition and the entrenchment of human rights. Many torts, including those associated with criminal acts, reflect violations of human rights such as the right to life, bodily integrity and property. That not all human rights violations are classified as torts should make no difference. Article 13 of the European Convention on Human rights assures a right to an effective remedy before a national authority to the victim of violations of his/her rights.

## X. Fair Trial

### 1. Requisites of a Fair Trial

We have already noted that the rights of the accused in criminal proceedings *28*
and generally of the litigant in any judicial proceedings, safeguarded by Article 12.5 and Article 30.3, are constituents or integral parts of a fair trial. The case law of the Supreme Court makes it clear that the rights of the accused and every litigant safeguarded by the Constitution are inseverable features of a fair trial. In *Yangou 'Lemonas' v. The Police (2001) 2 C.L.R. 421 (CA)*[156] the Supreme Court, adhering to earlier judicial authority, emphasized

[156] Judgment delivered by Pikis P.

that the rights assured to a litigant are an inseparable aspect of a fair trial. So, they voided the conviction of the appellant for breach of his right assured by Article 12.5c (corresponding to Article 6.3(c) of the European Convention on Human Rights) to have free legal assistance owing to lack of the necessary means. In *Carter v. Chief of the Police (1996) 1 C.L.R. 299 (FB)*[157] the Court underlined that the rights of the accused and every litigant are an incident of the freedom of man not to be withheld or denied at any time. The significance of the procedural rights of the accused for the individual is roundly identified by Justice Frankfurter in his judgment in *McNabb v. United States of America 87 Law Ed. 819* at p. 827: "The history of liberty has largely been the history of the observance of procedural safeguards".[158]

The determination of the civil rights and obligations of a person or any criminal charge against the individual becomes unfair if the trial is held contrary to or outside the norms of a fair trial stipulated for in Article 30.2 or the minimum rights of the accused or the litigant in a civil trial (see *Liassides a.o. v. The Police (2002) 2 C.L.R. 434 (CA)*[159]).

In *Gregoriou v. Bank of Cyprus (1992) 1 C.L.R. 1222 (CA)*[160] the judgment of a civil court was set aside and the trial declared to be abortive because the plaintiff was denied the opportunity to be present at his trial at the stage of final addresses. The notion of a fair trial entails, as the jurisprudence of the European Court of Human Rights[161] and the case law of the Supreme Court of Cyprus support, the right of the litigant to be present at his/her trial. And insofar as the trial court had unjustifiably refused an application of the plaintiff for adjournment on grounds of illness depriving him of the right to be present at his trial, the proceedings were found to be a nullity and a retrial of the case was ordered (see also *Kyriakos G. Kyriakides Ltd. v. Lumian Ltd. a.o. (2000) 2 C.L.R. 343 (CA)*[162]).

---

[157] Judgment delivered by Pikis P.

[158] Reference is made to the above extract form the judgment of Frankfurter J. in the dissenting opinion of Pikis P. in Papaioannou v. Papaioannou and Kolaridou v. Kolarides, (2000) 1 C.L.R 656.

[159] Judgment delivered by Pikis P.

[160] Judgment delivered by Pikis J.

[161] See G.E.F. Fawcett "The application of the European Convention on Human Rights"; Oxford: Clarendon Press, 1987.

[162] Judgment delivered by Pikis P.

The following are laid down by Article 30.2[163] as essential attributes of a fair trial:

The trial must be held before

a) a competent court set up by law; Article 30.1 prohibits the establishment of judicial committees or exceptional courts under any name whatsoever;
b) an independent and impartial court;
c) a court functioning in public unless the press and the public are excluded by a decision of the Court taken in the interest of (i) the security of the Republic (ii) constitutional order, (iii) public order, (iv) public safety, (v) public morals or (vi) where the interests of juveniles or the protection of the private life of the parties so require.

Furthermore, the proceedings must

a) be conducted within a reasonable time;
b) be concluded by a duly reasoned judgment.

2. A Duly Constituted Court

The Constitution provides for the establishment of superior courts and the setting up by law of subordinate courts in sufficient number for the proper and undelayed administration of justice and the efficient application of the provisions of the Constitution guaranteeing the fundamental rights and liberties of the person (Article 158.1). The terms and conditions of service of Judges of superior and subordinate courts shall not be altered to their disadvantage as the Constitution provides in Articles 153.11 and 158.3. *29*

Jurisdiction is vested in the Supreme Court to supervise subordinate courts with a view to ensuring that they operate within the bounds of their jurisdiction and in accordance with the rules of natural justice. This jurisdiction was inherited from English law and is exercised in much the same way

[163] It reads: In the determination of his civil rights and obligations or of any criminal charge against him, every person is entitled to a fair and public hearing within a reasonable time by an independent, impartial and competent court established by law. Judgment shall be reasoned and pronounced in public session, but the press and the public may be excluded from all or any part of the trial upon a decision of the court where it is in the interest of the security of the Republic or the constitutional order or the public order or the public safety or the public morals or where the interests of juveniles or the protection of the private life of the parties so require or, in special circumstances where, in the opinion of the court, publicity would prejudice the interests of justice.

that the High Court of England supervised inferior courts through the prerogative writs of certiorari, prohibition, mandamus and quo warranto. The Supreme Court is likewise empowered by the provisions of Article 155.4 to issue writs of certiorari, prohibition, mandamus and quo warranto.

The following extract from the decision of the Supreme Court in *re Kakos (1985) 1 C.L.R. 250*[164] highlights the nature of the corrective jurisdiction of the Supreme Court over the judicial process through the writ of certiorari:

> Certiorari lies primarily to ensure that an inferior Court operates within the bounds of its jurisdiction and observes fundamental rules of law.[165] In answering the plea relevant to jurisdiction, the test is whether the order made was within the jurisdiction of the Court that issued it. The absence of competence, if any, must be apparent on the record of the proceedings, as well as the illegality, manifest, as alleged. The process is intended to subject to scrutiny the assumption of jurisdiction and the legality of the order made, as opposed to its correctness.

## 3. An Independent Court

*30* The appointment, promotion and terms of service of Judges are of paramount importance for the independence of the Judiciary. The principle of separation of powers requires the separateness of the Judiciary from the other two branches of government in all respects. The institutional and functional independence of the courts lies at the heart of the independence of the Judiciary. Institutional independence of Judges has to do with the appointment of Judges and the terms and conditions of their service; whereas functional independence requires unfettered freedom in the discharge of their duties. The insurance against changes in their salaries and terms and conditions of service of Judges to their detriment after appointment enshrined in the Constitution constitutes one of the safeguards of their independence. The provisions of Article 166.1(b) making the salaries of Judges of the Supreme Court a permanent charge on the consolidated fund, obviating the need for annual provision for the payment of their salaries in the budget, is another attribute of their independence.

The appointment, promotion, transfer and discipline of Judges of subordinate courts are exclusively in the power of the Supreme Council of

---

164 Judgments delivered by A Loizou J. and Pikis J.

165 In re HjiCosta (1984) 1 C.L.R. 513, 517

Judicature consisting of all the Judges of the Supreme Court. As the case law of the Supreme Court establishes, no power of the State other than the Judiciary can participate directly or indirectly in the appointment, promotion or any matter affecting the status of judges. In the case of *Keramourgia "Aias" Ltd. v. Yiannakis Christoforou (1975) 1 C.L.R. 38 (FB)*[166] the Court held that the provisions of the Annual Holidays with Pay Law (L-8/67) regulating the appointment of the Chairman of the Arbitration Tribunal[167] were unconstitutional because they envisaged the involvement of the Executive in its making, violating thereby Article 157.2 as well as the doctrine of separation of powers. In *Pastellopoulos v. Republic (1985) 2 C.L.R. 165 (FB)*,[168] a majority decision, for similar reasons, the provisions of the Military Criminal Code and Procedure Law (L-40/64) providing for the appointment of the President and Deputy President of the Military Court by the Council of Ministers were held to be unconstitutional. The nomination of the lay members of the court (Officers of the National Guard) by the Commander of the force was held to be objectionable for like reasons. The Court explained that the independence of Judges assured by Article 30.2 requires independence of the court from the Executive and the parties. The relevant provisions of the law were also found to be incompatible with Article 157.2 entrusting the appointment of judges (of subordinate courts) to the Judiciary and violative of the principle of separation of powers. On the other hand, in *Poyiatzis v. Pilavakis a.o. (1986) 1 C.L.R. 47 (CA)*[169] the composition of the Rent Control Court was found to be innocuous since all the members of the Court, the judges and lay-members participating in the fact finding process, were appointed by the Supreme Council of Judicature.

As earlier noted, Judges of the Supreme Court are appointed by the President of the Republic. In the interest of the independence of the Judiciary a constitutional practice was evolved whereby in making appointments to the Supreme Court the President invariably seeks, and as a rule follows, the advice of the Supreme Court as to who should be appointed. The Judges nominated come from the ranks of the senior judiciary of the District Courts (Presidents of District Courts).

---

166 Judgment delivered by Triantafyllides P.

167 Subsequently renamed Labour Disputes Court.

168 Majority judgment delivered by Stylianides J, minority judgment delivered by A. Loizou J.

169 Judgment delivered by Pikis J, A. Loizou J. and Demetriades J.

4. An Impartial Court

31 The test of impartiality of the court is objective. Liberty is acknowledged to a Judge to excuse him/herself from the composition of the court of which he/she is a member whenever the Judge deems this to be in the interests of justice (see *President of the Republic v. House of Representatives (1985) 3 C.L.R. 1501 (P)*[170] and *Mavrogenis v. House of Representatives (No. 1) (1996) 1 C.L.R. 857 (P)*[171]). Self-exclusion apart, the court will not address a question of bias of a Judge unless it is raised by one or both of the parties to the case. If a Judge has a degree of connection with the case or the parties or an interest be it remote in the outcome of a case that does not in his view disqualify him/her to participate in the trial of the case, the proper course is to disclose the relevant facts affording the parties thereby the opportunity to raise objection to his/her sitting in the case. If objection is raised on grounds of bias, the Court will address the issue itself and resolve the matter before proceeding further in the case (see *Liassides (1999) 1 C.L.R. 185 (FB)*[172]).

The following extract from the decision in *Makrides v. Republic (1984) 3 C.L.R. 304 (SJ)*[173] characterizes the approach of the Court to a plea of disqualification:

> As I perceive my duty, in the absence of valid reasons disqualifying me from sitting in the case, to excuse myself would be an abdication of duty; an abdication of duty with visible dangers to the administration of justice. One such danger is that we would be coming close to acknowledging to a litigant a right to choose the Judge who will try him. I could neither condone such a practice nor shut off from my mind the repercussions from any such decision. It is not permissible to be merely guided by sentiment.

Reference to the principles emerging from the above case is made with approval by the majority in *Autocephalous Church of Cyprus v. House of Representatives (1990) 3 C.L.R. 54 (P).*[174]

32 The yardstick for determination of bias on the part of the court is the reaction of a reasonable man acquainted with the facts relevant to the "interest of the Judge in the case". If the reaction of such a person would be that no

[170] Judgment delivered by Triantafyllides P.
[171] Judgment delivered by Pikis P.
[172] Judgment delivered by Pikis P.
[173] Judgment delivered by Pikis J.
[174] Majority judgment delivered by A. Loizou P., minority judgment delivered by Stylianides J.

fair trial could be held, then disqualification applies. In *Economides v. Police a.o. (1983) 2 C.L.R. 301 (CA)*[175] the Supreme Court ruled that a Judge dealing with an application for the remand of a suspect in custody cannot be deemed to be biased against the suspect merely on account of the fact that he dealt with a similar application against the same person on a previous occasion. Remand in custody does not involve findings of credibility of witnesses or the suspect. For similar reasons, in *Pantelis Vrakas a.o. v. Republic (1973) 2 C.L.R. 139 (FB)*[176] the Supreme Court ruled there was no impediment to a Judge who held a preliminary inquiry into the justification of committing the accused to trial before the Assize Court sitting as a member of the Assize Court that tried the case. The test for committing a person to trial before the Assize Court is wholly impersonal tied to the objective implications of the evidence available against the accused.

A judicial decision on a question of law is no bar to a Judge sitting in another case involving determination of the same or a similar question of law.[177] A Judge cannot be charged with having an "interest" in appearing to be infallible. Not only before the trial but also during the trial the Judge must strenuously avoid leaving an impression of partiality. In the case of *Bank of Cyprus Ltd. v. Dynacon Ltd. a.o (1999) 1 C.L.R. 717 (CA)*[178] the Supreme Court set aside the decision of the arbitrators, a body exercising inherently judicial duties, because one of them made, after the conclusion of the case and reservation of judgment, a comment to a director of the defendant company outside the court to the effect that their case was a waste of time. The Supreme Court observed that such conduct was unbefitting (unbecoming) a person exercising judicial duties. Judges must conduct themselves in a manner compatible with the requisites of impartiality and the impersonal character of the judicial process. Departure from these standards tends to undermine faith in the Judges and the institutions of justice casting doubts on the impartiality of the court. The case of *Evangelou a.o. v. Ambizas a.o. (1982) 1 C.L.R. 41 (CA)*[179] is instructive as to how judges should conduct themselves in the exercise of judicial duties:

> Although a judge may intervene in order to ensure that the proceedings follow the course ordained by the rules of evidence and procedure, he must avoid

[175] Judgment delivered by A. Loizou J.
[176] Judgment delivered by Triantafyllides P.
[177] Vassiliades v. Vassiliades 18 C.L.R. 10
[178] Judgment delivered by Pikis P.
[179] Judgment delivered by Pikis J.

interfering beyond the limits indicated above, and especially refrain from passing unnecessary comments that may create the impression of descending into the arena of the trial. A judge must invariably distance himself from the conflict that unfolds before him and maintain strictly his arbitral position throughout the proceedings (see *Jones v. National Coal Board [1957] 2 All E.R. 155 and Yianni v. Yianni [1966] 1 All E.R. 231*). Any departure from this stance of aloofness may compromise, in the eyes of the litigant, as well as third parties, his impartiality.

Discourtesy on the part of the Judge cannot be countenanced in the conduct of judicial proceedings. The following was said on the subject in the case of *Shacolas v. Universal Life (1984) 1 C.L.R. 47 (CA)*[180]:

> Nothing said in this judgment should be construed as condoning discourtesy on the part of judges to counsel or anyone for that matter – witnesses or members of the public. Discourtesy lowers the dignity of the Court and may weaken confidence in the patience of the Judiciary to transact judicial business in a climate of calm essential for the administration of justice. Patience combined with firmness are the two essential attributes for robust judgmentship.

Judicial propriety in the conduct of the judicial proceedings is a consequential factor for the good administration of justice. In *Silvestrou v. Police (1996) 2 C.L.R. 159 (CA)*[181] the Supreme Court stressed that descending into the arena of conflict tends to undermine the appearance of impartiality of the Court.

*33* The impartiality of the Court may be tainted by factors extraneous to the proceedings poisoning the climate in which the trial is held. Publications tending to prejudge the outcome of a case or prejudicial to a party to judicial proceedings and more so stigmatisation of litigants tend to pollute the climate in which justice is administered. In *Constantinides v. Vima Ltd. a.o. (1983) 1 C.L.R. 348 (CA)*[182] the Supreme Court declared that trial by the press is antinomous to and undermines the foundations of justice. The principle enshrined in Article 30.2 requires that the sole arbiters of the criminal responsibility and the civil rights and obligations of litigants shall be the courts of law of the Republic. Prejudicial statements defy the rights of the litigants to a fair trial and tend to undermine the Judiciary as the constitutional

[180] Judgment delivered by Pikis J.
[181] Judgment delivered by Kallis J.
[182] Judgment delivered by Pikis J.

guardian of the rights of the individual. The right to a fair trial is interwoven with the right to freedom; in essence indistinguishable from freedom itself. In *Ellinas v. Republic (1989) 2 C.L.R. 149 (CA)*[183] the Supreme Court recalled the aphorism of Lord Hardwicke in *St. James Evenings Post Case*[184] that nothing is of greater significance for freedom than the keeping of the stream of justice unpolluted so that everyone can have recourse to the court without fear of consequences for his person or his reputation. In *Ellinas* (supra) the Supreme Court indicated that the dicta of Lord Hardwicke accurately reflect the relationship between man, justice and society generally. Generating prejudice against a litigant, the Court said, defies not only the right to a fair trial but the mission of the Judiciary as the sole arbiter of the rights of man too. On the other hand, we must not overlook that the likelihood of the Court being biased on account of prejudicial atmosphere surrounding the case because of press reports or adverse comments, is far smaller when the Court is composed solely of professional judges responsible for deciding both questions of law and fact in the case (see *Police v. Phanti a.o. (1994) 2 C.L.R. 160 (CA)*[185]).

5. Public Hearing

The hearing of a case must be held in public. In *Michail a.o. v. Poullou* 34
*Brothers Ltd. (2001) 1 C.L.R. 438 (CA)*[186] the Court deprecated the hearing of an application in the Chambers of a judge and not in open court.

The Court must ensure that the rights of the accused safeguarded by Article 12.5 and 30.3 are heeded and given effect to throughout the trial. In *Liassidis a.o. v. The Police (2002) 2 C.L.R. 434 (CA)*[187] the decision of the trial court in a criminal case of indecent assault was set aside because the accused was denied the opportunity to cross-examine a witness for the prosecution.[188] The witness had left the country and for that reason her statement was produced in court pursuant to the provisions of Section 4(2) of the Evidence Law CAP 9; a law that was in force at the time of independence.

---

183 Judgment delivered by Pikis J.

184 St. James Evenings Post (1742) 2 Atk. 469.

185 Majority judgment delivered by Artemides J, minority judgment delivered by Constantinides J.

186 Judgment delivered by Pikis P.

187 Judgment delivered by Pikis. J.

188 The statement of the witness was produced after the close of the case for the defence in relation to a subject that arose ex improviso.

The Court set aside the conviction for inter alia breach of the right of the accused to examine a witness of the adversary. The Court found the pre-independence law authorizing the course adopted by the trial court to be incompatible with the Constitution and for that reason inapplicable after independence. The right to a public hearing requires that evidence be heard in public. A public hearing assures the open administration of justice, a course in which the public too has a vital interest. We may remind that the right to examine witnesses according to law is also assured to litigants in civil proceedings.

The decision in *Liassides v. The Police* (supra) was not followed in the case of *A. Panayides Contracting Ltd. v. Charalambous (2004) 1 C.L.R. 416 (P) (majority decision)*.[189] A bill of medical expenses for treatment received abroad (in the United Kingdom) based on hospital records was found to be admissible in view of the difficulty to secure the attendance of witnesses residing abroad. In this connection, the majority followed the trend of the case law of the European Court of Human Rights to the effect that the right to confront witnesses is not absolute, admitting exceptions where the interests of justice are not at risk.[190] In the view of the majority, the provisions of Section 4(2) of the Evidence Law making admissible the statement of witnesses who are abroad and cannot attend are not ruled out by Article 30.3 (c) of the Constitution (assuring a right to examine witnesses according to law). At the least, this is the position in civil cases. Another strand of the majority view shared by three Justices is that the right to confrontation of witnesses differs in criminal as opposed to civil cases. In the case of Article 6.3(d) of the European Convention on Human Rights the right to confrontation in criminal cases is laid down in the following terms: "to examine or have examined witnesses against him".

The minority adopted *Liassides v. The Police* (supra) as a matter of precedent. Its ratio is warranted, as they noted, not only be the provisions of Article 12.3(d) and Article 30.3(c) but by the requisites of a fair trial.[191]

[189] Majority decisions delivered by Artemides J., Constantinides J., Nicolaou J., Gavrielidis J. and Hadjihambis J.; minority decisions delivered by Pikis P. and Kallis J.

[190] See inter alia Case of Beckels v. The United Kingdom Application No. 44652/98, 8th October 2002; Case of Luca v. Italy Application No. 33354/96, 27th February 2001; Case of P.S. v. Germany Application No. 33900/96, 20th December 2001.

[191] See inter alia Case of Kostovski v. The Netherlands Application No. 11454/85, 20th November 1989; Case of Windisch v. Austria Application No. 12489/86, 27th September 1990; Case of Dombo Beheer BV v. The Netherlands Application No. 14448/88, 27th October1993; Case of Vidal v. Belgium Application No. 12351/86, 22nd April 1992.

The term "witness" ("martiras" in Greek) denotes according to the dictionary meaning of the word, a person who certifies or describes a fact of which he/she is aware of before a judicial authority. A kindred meaning is ascribed to the word "witness" in the context of the European Convention on Human Rights in the case law of the European Court of Human Rights.[192]

On the right of confrontation reference may be made to a recent decision of the Federal Supreme Court of the United States of America (see *Crawford v. Washington 541 U.S. 36, 124 S. Ct. 1354 (2004))*. The Federal Supreme Court decided that the right assured to a person by the Sixth Amendment "... to be confronted with witnesses against him ..." admits of no exceptions. It applies equally to testimonial and non-testimonial hearsay evidence.[193]

## 6. Reasoning of Judicial Decisions

The judgment of the court must be reasoned. This is an indispensable element of a fair trial. What are the attributes of a duly reasoned judgment? To answer the question, the judgment must be examined as a whole. In *Pioneer Candy Ltd. v. Tryfon and Sons (1981) 1 C.L.R. 540 (CA)*[194] the Court sought to identify the elements of a duly reasoned judgment in a civil case. It must contain: *35*

a) And analysis of the evidence adduced in the light of the issues as arising an defined by the pleadings;
b) Concrete findings as the necessary prelude to the judgment of the Court; and
c) A clear judicial pronouncement indicating the outcome of the case (*Theodora Ioannidou v. Charilaos Dikeos (1969) 1 C.L.R 235*[195]).

The issues of a criminal trial are defined by the charges and the answer of the accused to them. If a plea of not-guilty is entered, everything relevant to the proof of the charge is put in issue.

---

192 See Case of Lüdi v. Switzerland 12433/86, 15th June 1992.

193 In so holding, the Federal Supreme Court overruled a previous decision of the Federal Supreme Court, Ohio v. Roberts 448 U.S. 56 (1980), a view not shared by two of the nine Justices of the Federal Supreme Court.

194 Judgment delivered by Loris J.

195 Judgment delivered by Vassiliades P.

In *Glyky v. Municipality of Limasol (1998) 1 C.L.R. 2319 (CA)*[196] an order of the trial court was set aside for inter alia lack of due reasoning as the judgment of the court was confined to recording the outcome of the case without reference to the reasons founding it. Likewise in *Paphitis & Iordanous Contractors Ltd a.o. v. A. N. Stassis Estates Ltd. (1998) 1 C.L.R. 916 (CA)*[197] the judgment of the trial court was voided and retrial was ordered as it recorded nothing other than the conclusions of the court. The importance of reasoning and the implications of failure to provide it are articulated in the extract cited below from *Neophytou v. The Police (1981) 2 C.L.R. 195 (CA)*[198]:

> The supply of proper reasoning for the deliberations of the Court, particularly the reasons for the conviction of the accused, is mandatorily warranted by the Constitution, notably Article 30.2, and constitutes at the same time a fundamental attribute of the judicial process. In the longer run, faith in the Judiciary of the State and its mission depends, to a very large extent, on the persuasiveness of the reasons given by the Courts in support of their decisions. Any laxity in this area would inevitably undermine faith in the premises of justice. The need for proper reasoning is not only warranted by the interests of the litigants but also by the interests of the general public in the proper administration of justice. The impression of arbitrariness is the one element that must constantly be kept well outside the sphere of judicial deliberations.

The reasoning of judicial decisions is, it may be said, a species of accountability for judicial action.

### 7. Trial within a Reasonable Time

*36* The aphorism "justice delayed is justice denied" accurately reflects the consequences of delay in the administration of justice. The dispensation of justice within a reasonable time is incorporated in Article 30.2 as a necessary element of a fair trial. In *Agapiou v. Panayiotou (1988) 1 C.L.R. 257 (CA)*[199] the Court proclaimed:

> Justice delayed is justice denied. This aphorism must be in the forefront of judicial thought and actions.

[196] Judgment delivered by Pikis P.
[197] Judgment delivered by Pikis P.
[198] Judgment delivered by Pikis J.
[199] Judgment delivered by Pikis J.

Reasonableness of the length of the proceedings is not decided in abstracto but by reference to the facts and circumstances of the case, particularly its complexity and the conduct of the parties relevant to the discharge of their duty to present their case before the court. In *Paporis v. National Bank of Greece (1986) 1 C.L.R. 578 (CA)*[200] the Court explained that the need to conclude the proceedings within a reasonable time is not a rule of prescription (limitation of action) but a fundamental principle of the administration of justice. In civil proceedings time begins to run from the date the actions is initiated.

In a criminal case time begins to run from the date of the arrest of the accused or the date of the lodgement of the complaint against him/her, whichever is the earliest (see inter alia *Ellinas* (supra) and *Kafkaris v. Republic (1990) 2 C.L.R. 203 (CA)*[201]). A case must be investigated without delay. As early as the investigation is completed and a case is disclosed against the accused, it is the duty of the prosecuting authority to lay charges before the Court. In *M & M Loizou Ltd a.o. v. Jumbo Investments Ltd. (2000) 2 C.L.R. 717 (CA)*[202] the Court stressed that the prosecution of the offenders as early as their criminal conduct comes to light is a component of the due and fair administration of justice.

The reasonableness of the time within which a trial is concluded is in the nature 37
of things linked to the volume of evidence in support of the case of either party, the complexity of the issues arising for consideration and the conduct of the parties. Litigants responsible for delays in the conduct of the proceedings cannot legitimately complain about them. However, it is the bounden duty of the Court to ensure that cases are tried within a reasonable time.

In *Victoros v. Christodoulou (1992) 1 C.L.R. 512 (CA)*[203] the Court underlined that the value of the rights of man is directly dependent upon the efficacy of the mechanisms for their protection and the time within which justice bears fruition. The timely administration of justice constitutes an element of justice itself. As much is declared to be the case in the first charter of human rights in the modern era, namely the Magna Carta of 1215, wherein it is proclaimed that delay in the administration of justice constitutes a denial of it. In *Victoros* (supra) the judgment of the trial court

[200] Judgments delivered by Justices A. Loizou, Savvides and Pikis.
[201] Judgment delivered by Pikis J.
[202] Judgment delivered by Pikis P.
[203] Judgment delivered by Pikis J.

was set aside because of the inordinate delay of the Court in giving judgment after the conclusion of the proceedings.

In *Efstathiou v. Police (1990) 2 C.L.R. 294 (CA)*[204] the conviction of the accused for driving without due care and attention was quashed because his criminal responsibility was determined outside the span of reasonable time. The offence was reported on 13th October 1987, the accused was summoned before the Court eleven months later; thereafter the case was adjourned twice on account of lack of preparedness on the part of the prosecution. The trial was concluded on 3rd January 1990. Annulling the judgment of the trial court for straying outside the parameters of a fair trial, the Court indicated that the interval that elapsed between the reporting of the case and the outcome of the proceedings was unreasonably long. In *Christopoulos v. Police (2001) 2 C.L.R. 100 (CA)*[205] the accused appealed his conviction on 12 charges of theft by agent complaining inter alia that his trial was not concluded within a reasonable time and for that reason it was unfair. The case had been repeatedly adjourned at the instance of the prosecution and on a good number of occasions by the court itself for lack of time to deal with the case on the appointed day. It took six years before the trial was concluded. The trial of the case, the Court observed, was allowed to linger on regardless of time and the duty to conclude it within a reasonable time. Determination of the criminal liability of the accused to a charge within a reasonable time is a fundamental right of the individual and a foremost duty of the State to ensure. In the result, the trial was found not to have been fair, the convictions were set aside and the accused was discharged. No retrial was ordered because the time that had elapsed made retrial within a reasonable time impossible.

## 8. The Context within which the Rights of the Accused or a Litigant are Exercised

*38* The rights of the litigant must be exercised within the context of the trial and for the purpose they are designed to serve that is to ensure a fair trial. The unimpeded administration of justice is one of the cornerstones of constitutional order and a guarantee for the sustenance of the rights of man. The administration of justice cannot be subordinated to or be interrupted by any reason extraneous to the purposes it is designed to serve, its purpose

[204] Judgment delivered by Pikis J.
[205] Judgment delivered by Pikis J.

being to minister justice. In *Rousos a.o. v. Republic (1984) 3 C.L.R. 1437 (SJ)*[206] the Court refused to adjourn a case owing to the absence of counsel of a litigant due to strike action by lawyers. In *Fourri a.o. v. Republic (1980) 2 C.L.R. 152 (CA)*[207] the Court pointed out that the rights of the accused and the litigant generally, safeguarded respectively by Articles 12.5 and 30.3, cannot be divorced from the framework or the objects of a trial. The accused or the litigant in civil proceedings cannot exercise his/her rights in a manner contradictory to the objectives of a trial embodied in the norms of a fair trial.[208] The extract below from the decision in *King's Head Development Co. Ltd v. Pylea (2001) 1 C.L.R. 733 (CA)*[209] reflects the approach of the Court to the subject: "The rights of the litigant are safeguarded so long as they are exercised within the context of the judicial process and not outside it or contrary to its objectives".[210] The rights of the litigants must be exercised in a manner consistent with a fair trial and not in a way antithetical to its purposes. In *Efthymiou (1987) 1 C.L.R. 329 (SJ)*[211] the question the Court had to answer was whether a witness is incapacitated to act as the lawyer of the litigant who called him to testify. The Court held that the lawyer, an officer of justice under the Advocates Law CAP 2, was incapacitated from acting as the lawyer in the case. The Court pointed out that the incapacitation of the lawyer to act for her client stemmed from the exercise of another fundamental right of the litigant namely the right to call witnesses in support of her case. The following passage from the judgment of the Court provides an answer to reconciling competing rights of a person "where fundamental rights are interwoven with the judicial process, they must be interpreted and applied in a way harmonising constitutional objectives".

So long as the rights of the accused or the litigant are exercised within the context of the rules governing the holding of a fair trial, their exercise cannot be fettered (see *Kittis v. Michaelides a.o. (No. 2) (2000) 1 C.L.R. 1915 (CA)*[212]).

---

206 Judgment delivered by Pikis J.

207 Judgments delivered by A. Loizou J and Triantafyllides P.

208 see Mangakis (1990) 1 C.L.R. 1068; Christodoulou (1991) 1 C.L.R. 34; King's Head Development Co Ltd v. Pylea (2001) 1 C.L.R. 733.

209 Judgment delivered by Pikis P.

210 Translation from Greek.

211 Judgment delivered by Pikis J.

212 Judgment delivered by Pikis P.

9. Consequences of Breach of the Norms of a Fair Trial

39 Deviation from the norms of a fair trial derails the process entailing the voidance of the proceedings. The Supreme Court has consistently adopted the position that breach of or deviation from the norms of a fair trial renders the proceedings abortive and for that reason indeterminate as to the civil rights and obligations or criminal responsibility of the litigant. In *Efstathiou* (supra) the Court drew attention to the fact that Article 30.2 defines the prerequisites for a valid determination of the civil rights and obligations of a party to civil proceedings and the criminal responsibility of an accused in a criminal trial. Analogous to *Efstathiou* (supra) was the approach of the Supreme Court in *Victoros v. Christodoulou* (supra) as to the consequences that breach of the requisites of a fair trial entails.[213]

The holding of a fair trial and evaluation of the consequences of departure therefrom are assessed within the context of the trial in its entirety, as a rule at the end of the day.[214] Breach of the principles of fair trial nullifies the proceedings. The decision of the court is set aside. The process to fill the gap is through a retrial of the case provided there is no obstacle to holding a fair trial which may be the case if the interval of time that elapsed renders trial within a reasonable time impossible.[215]

40 The principles emerging from the jurisprudence of the Supreme Court respecting a fair trial and consequences of breach of or deviation from its requisites may be summed up as follows:

a) A fair trial is the only avenue for the determination of the civil rights and obligations or the criminal responsibility of a person.
b) A fair trial is one held in accordance with the principles laid down in Article 30.2 and 3 and coincidentally Article 12.5 in criminal proceedings.
c) Deviation from the norms of a fair trial renders the proceedings a nullity necessitating the retrial of a case unless this ceases to be an option owing to the lapse of time.

[213] see also Yangou "Lemonas" v. The Police (supra).
[214] See Republic v. Ford (No. 2) (1995) 2 C.L.R. 232.
[215] see Christopoulos v. Police (supra).

# F

# Separation of Powers: The Sphere and Authority of Each One of the Three Powers of the State

## I. Separation of Powers – The Principle and its Application Under the Constitution

The Constitution of Cyprus is founded on the principle of separation of powers. The sphere, competence and jurisdiction of each one of the three powers of the State and matters incidental thereto are earmarked in separate Parts of the Constitution. *1*

Each one of the three powers of the State, the Legislature, the Executive and the Judiciary, is invested with power to act over the entire field of action covered by the corresponding domain of authority except to the extent that provision to the contrary is made in the Constitution.

Article 61 assigns the legislative power of the Republic in all matters (other than matters expressly reserved for the Communal Chambers) to the House of Representatives.

Article 54 entrusts executive power to the Council of Ministers in all matters other than those specified below assigned to other organs of the Executive:

a) Executive power reserved for the President or Vice-President of the Republic under Articles 47, 48 and 49, and
b) Executive power expressly reserved for the Communal Chambers.

Articles 136 and 152 trust the judicial power of the State to the Supreme Constitutional Court on the one hand and the High Court and courts subordinate thereto, established by law, on the other.

Article 35 heeds the separation between the spheres of authority of the three powers of the State enjoining each one of them to ensure within the limits of their respective competence the efficient application of human rights, the subject of Part II of the Constitution. The three powers of the State are often portrayed as branches of the same trunk, the State.

## 1. The Legislature

2 In juridical terms, the legislative power embraces law-making, i.e. the establishment of rules regulating the affairs of man (in all walks of life) and rules for the governance of the country. Such rules must have a normative character and be of general application, conferring rights, imposing duties, defining obligations or establishing the parameters of public administration. Such rules must be impersonal in character, the hallmark of legislative acts. Personalized legislation smacks of administrative or executive action, the province of the Executive.

Aristotle represents law as the neutral authority to which everyone seeking justice may apply.

In *President of the Republic v. House of Representatives (1992) 3 C.L.R. 109 (P) (majority judgment)*[215] legislation prohibiting the use of an area approved by the Executive for the dumping of refuse was declared unconstitutional. Its provisions lacked the attributes of law. Disposal of refuse and matters associated therewith belonged to the domain of the Administration. What the Legislature sought to effect was to override action of the Executive in a matter lying solely within the latter's sphere of authority. The measure adopted was an act of public administration enacted in breach of the principle of separation of powers.

[215] Majority judgment delivered by Pikis J, minority judgment delivered by A Loizou J.

### 2. The Executive

The executive power derives its name from its principal function that lies in the execution of laws. Its sphere of authority is not confined to that area only. It extends to the control of the machinery of government. In its exclusive domain lie foreign affairs, security and defence. 3

### 3. The Judiciary

The resolution of disputes between members of the public or members of the public and public authorities or between public authorities by reference to law as well as the adjudication upon conflicts respecting the authority of organs of government prescribe the parameters of judicial power. Courts of law are the vestees of the judicial power of the State trusted with jurisdiction to adjudicate upon every dispute or question referable to the rights and obligations of the parties, to determine the criminal responsibility of a person to a charge and to provide an authoritative interpretation of the law with a view to avoiding the eruption of impending conflicts. 4

## II. Functional Separation between Political and Administrative Authorities

The Constitution introduces yet another species of separation of powers, namely separation between the political and administrative authorities of the State. The Constitution entrusts the manning (appointment, promotion, transfer and discipline) of the public service to an independent body, the Public Service Commission (Article 122). The terms and conditions of service of its members are assimilated to those of Judges of the Supreme Court. After their appointment their remuneration cannot be altered to their disadvantage. They enjoy for the duration of their appointment security of tenure like Judges of the Supreme Court. Their service cannot be terminated except for like reasons to those governing the termination of the service of Judges of the Supreme Court and by the same body, that is by the same judicial council in judicial proceedings. 5

A Minister is a member of the Executive exercising executive power over and in relation to the Ministry that he/she heads. The powers of a Minister are laid down in Article 58. The authority of a Minister extends to all subjects relating to the execution of laws referable to the Department of State over which he/she presides and the administrative process associated therewith.

The Minister is empowered to issue directions and give instructions for the carrying out of the provisions of any law affecting the Ministry and of any order or regulation made under such law. Ministers have no power or authority over the staffing of the Ministry nor do they exercise any disciplinary authority over personnel. Civil servants have a permanent and diachronic mandate to administer according to law. The fate of the government in power is not and ought not to be their concern.

The separation between political and administrative authorities was acknowledged in the case of *Charilaos Frangoulides (No. 2) v. The Republic of Cyprus through the Public Service Commission (1966) 3 C.L.R. 676 (FB)*[216] and many subsequent decisions. In the above case, the participation of the Minister, assuming the authority of the Head of the Department, in the preparation of the annual confidential report as to the value of the services of the applicant was found to be outside his sphere of authority. And inasmuch as this report, unfavourable for the applicant, materially affected the decision of the Public Service Commission not to promote him, the decision was voided on grounds of unconstitutionality. The Court drew attention to the fact that Article 59.2 makes the holding of a Ministerial position and other political offices incompatible with the position of a civil servant and vice versa. There can be no admixture of the functions of the two offices. The assignment of appointments and promotions of public servants to an independent and autonomous body underlines the constitutional principle of separation between political office and public service.

*6* This separation between the political and administrative wings of the Executive is meant to secure the neutrality of the public service with regard to the aspirations of the government in power and generally remove every semblance of politicization of its mission. Civil servants serve the law not the government of the day. This separation best accords with the principle of equality embodied in Article 28. It tends to remove every shadow of political bias on the part of public servants in the discharge of their duties.[217] A report tending to disclose under the guise of a character report the political orientations of candidates for appointment to the public service was denounced as inadmissible in *Papantoniou a.o. v. Public Service Commission (1983) 3 C.L.R. 64 (SJ)*.[218] Such devices tend to pollute the process of selection with political bias that should not be countenanced.

---

[216] Judgment delivered by Vassiliades P.

[217] See Frangoulides v. Republic (1982) 1 C.L.R. 462.

[218] Judgment delivered by Pikis J.

Ministers are politically accountable for their service, whereas public servants are disciplinarily accountable for the discharge of their duties. The political neutrality of the civil service is a potent factor for the sustenance of government under the law unaffected by the political processes of government.

In the case of *Cyprus Broadcasting Corporation a.o. v. Karayiorghis a.o. (1991) 3 C.L.R. 159 (P)*[219] the Supreme Court declared, by majority, unconstitutional a law providing for the presence of observers nominated by parliamentary political parties on the boards of public corporations (forming part of the public service under the Constitution) trusted inter alia with appointment, promotion and transfer of personnel. One of the reasons was breach of the principle of separation between the body politic and the public service. The law was declared unconstitutional for other reasons too; because it provided that parliamentary political parties would nominate members for appointment to the boards of public corporations with a corresponding duty cast upon the Council of Ministers to give effect to their recommendations, a process entailing breach of the separation between the executive and legislative powers. Furthermore, the law was declared unconstitutional on account of breach of the principle of equality assuring equal treatment by the Administration to every individual independently of political convictions or other preferences. In *Pavlou a.o. v. General Registrar of Elections (1987) 1 C.L.R. 252 (majority judgment)*[220] the Court debated at length the distinction between political and administrative authorities; political authorities determine policy, the public service administers according to law. A law rendering incompatible the holding of an elective office in the municipal council and a post in the public service was pronounced to be constitutional, rejecting submissions to the contrary. A civil servant elected to a municipal council could assume such office only upon relinquishing the position held in the public service.

The first Public Service Law (L-33/67) after independence prohibited civil 7
servants from belonging to political parties. This was ended by subsequent legislation. A new Public Service Law was enacted in 1990 (L-1/90), the constitutionality of the relevant provisions of which came up for consideration before the Supreme Court in *President of the Republic v. House of Representatives*

[219] Majority judgment delivered by Pikis J., minority judgment delivered by Stylianides J.

[220] Judgments delivered by Triantafyllides P, and Justices Malachtos, Stylianides, Pikis and Kourris.

*(1991) 3 C.L.R. 631 (P)*[221] and *President of the Republic v. House of Representatives (1991) 3 C.L.R. 683 (P) (majority judgment).*[222] The Court upheld (by majority) the constitutionality of the new law entitling civil servants of every rank to join political parties, treating the freedom to belong to a political party as an incident of the right of freedom of association guaranteed by Article 21.2. The minority held otherwise on the ground inter alia that the law breached the separation between political and administrative authorities enshrined in the Constitution. A second reason for which the law was found by the minority to be unconstitutional was breach of Article 28 guaranteeing equality of treatment by the Administration, requiring the absence of bias or colour of prejudice on the part of the Administration.

The neutrality in substance and appearance of those taking action or making decisions in the name of the law may be said to be one of the cornerstones of the principle of equality deeply rooted in Article 28. In the exercise of their duties, civil servants should be free from every constraint real or apparent both in relation to the treatment of subordinate personnel as well as with regard to addressing requests of citizens for the issuance of administrative acts or decisions. They must not only in substance but in appearance too act impersonally. Where the rights of individuals are the subject of a decision, the attributes of impartiality of decision makers must be manifest, beyond a shadow of bias.

## III. Classification of Competencies and Authority of the Powers of the State

8 The classification of powers for the purpose of ascertaining the respective domain of each of the three powers has been a subject repeatedly addressed by the Supreme Court. The principle emerging from the case law is that the intrinsic nature of a given competence is the denominator for its classification.

A competence involving the exercise of executive or administrative authority cannot emanate or derive from the legislative power under the guise of legislation. In *President of the Republic v. House of Representatives (1992) 3 C.L.R. 458 (P)*[223] a law purporting to extend the tenure of the serving members (five

[221] Majority judgment delivered by A. Loizou P., minority judgment delivered by Pikis J.

[222] Majority judgment delivered by A. Loizou P., minority judgment delivered by Pikis J.

[223] Judgment delivered by Stylianides J.

in number) of the Public Educational Service Commission was declared unconstitutional on the ground that the subject-matter of the law fell in the sphere of the Executive. By an amendment of the law governing educational service the Legislature sought to extend the tenure of serving members of the aforesaid Commission. Had the subject of the law been a redefinition of the tenure of members of the said body, the law would have been unobjectionable. It would have been an impersonal piece of legislation changing the norms affecting the tenure and terms of service of members of the Educational Service Commission, the offspring of statutory law. Had that been the aim of the law, it would have passed the test of constitutionality. But as it was, the law was a personalized piece of legislation designed to extend the tenure of serving members of an administrative organ, a matter outside the power of the Legislature. The legislation contained no legal norm.

The Constitution introduces certain exceptions to the doctrine of separa- 9
tion of powers noted below:

a) Power is conferred upon the Council of Ministers to consider bills to be introduced to the House of Representatives by a Minister (Article 54(f) and Article 80.1). This is a preparatory legislative act as acknowledged in *Police v. Theodoros Nicola Hondrou 3 R.S.C.C. 82.*[224]
b) Article 80.2 imposes a limitation upon the power of the House of Representatives to make laws to the extent that it prohibits the introduction by a Representative of a bill relating to an increase of budgetary expenditure. This is a generally acknowledged exception to the doctrine of separation of powers in recognition of the realities of financial management and the responsibility of the Executive for the finances of the State.
c) The right to prepare and submit the budget is confined to the Executive acting through the Minister of Finance (see Article 167). With regard to the approval of the budget, the power of the Legislature is further constrained by the fact that it may not increase the expenditure provided therein or alter the purpose to which it is allocated (Article 167.6). In *President of the Republic v. House of Representatives (1996) 3 C.L.R. 462 (P)*[225] the Supreme Court opined that a bill entails an increase in expenditure, if this is the natural corollary or the inevitable consequence of its adoption.

---

[224] Judgment of the Court read by Forsthoff P.
[225] Judgment delivered by Pikis P.

10 Separation of powers entails the equality of the powers of the State and their autonomy in their separate spheres of authority where they enjoy freedom to regulate their proceedings and processes. Rule making relevant to their functioning is in the power of each branch of the State, notwithstanding the regulatory nature of the function that would otherwise justify its characterisation as a legislative act.

In the case of the Judiciary, power is bestowed upon the Supreme Court to prescribe and regulate the composition of the registries of the courts as well as the powers and duties of their officers, functions having the attributes of executive power (see Article 163). By the same Article power is acknowledged to the Supreme Court to lay down the rules governing the exercise of the jurisdiction of courts of law.

11 In a system of separation of powers, each branch acts co-ordinately with the other branches of the State for the promotion and achievement of the constitutional goals and the purposes for which power is conferred upon each of them by law. In the case *Akinita Chr. Hadjikyriakos Ltd. v. Republic (2001) 2 C.L.R. 901 (P) (majority decision)*[226] the equality of the three powers of the State was identified as a central feature of the system of separation of powers. In the same case, reference was made to the intrinsic competencies inhering in each power.

Aristotle first proclaimed a system of separation of powers as essential for symmetrical rule. Montesquieu in the modern era took up the same theme in his work "Esprit des Lois". In his analysis of the doctrine of separation of powers great emphasis is laid on the independence and separateness of the Judiciary from the other powers of the State regarded as a dominant characteristic of a system of separation of powers. Guided by this understanding of separation of powers, he discerned that the doctrine found application in Great Britain on account of the independence of the Judiciary. It must however be noted, its independence was not constitutionally entrenched, nor were its competencies, jurisdiction and powers unchangeably assured. The fundamental norm of the unwritten English Constitution is that Parliament is supreme. In its supremacy, Parliament may expand or restrict the judicial domain.

[226] Majority decision delivered by Pikis P., minority decision delivered by Nikitas J.

12 It can be persuasively argued that the principle of separation of powers requires the attribution of the totality of the competencies, jurisdiction and powers falling as of their nature in the domain of each power to the corresponding authorities charged with the exercise of such competence. The object of separation of powers is to ensure that State authority is exercised, depending on its nature, by the authority of the State entrusted with that part of State power. Selective assignment of powers to the three branches of the State is a derogation from the principle of separation of powers antagonistic to its objectives, undermining the effectiveness of a system of checks and balances that lies at the root of the doctrine of separation of powers. By separating the powers of the State, the supremacy of the law is best assured through the entrustment of the interpretation and application of the law to a neutral authority, the Judiciary, unassociated with the promotion of any ends other than those of the law itself. The distribution of State power among the three pillars of the State according to its character constitutes the foundation stone of the principle of separation of powers. Allocation of power according to this order is best assured through a supreme law such as the Constitution or a basic law entrenching such distribution as a salient aspect of constitutional order. The ultimate guardian of this order is the Judiciary, in whose power it should be to declare laws, acts or omissions contrary to it unconstitutional.

## IV. The Domain of the Judiciary

13 The interpretation of law is the exclusive province of the Judiciary. The Legislature makes the law but has no right to interpret it. An attempt to do so was struck down as unconstitutional in *Diagoras Development Ltd. v. National Bank of Greece S.A. (1985) 1 C.L.R. 581 (CA) (majority decision)*[227]. Certainty about the law would be shaken if anyone other than the Judiciary was entrusted to interpret it, ascribing to it such meaning as its wording viewed in context warrants.

Unless constrained by the Constitution, the Legislature may change the law retrospectively. The only restriction is to be found in Article 24.3 prohibiting the retrospective imposition of taxes, duties or rates of any kind.

[227] Majority concurring judgments delivered by Triantafyllides P. and Justices Loris, Pikis and Kourris.

In *Diagoras Development* (supra) the Court followed the earlier decision *Malachtou v. Attorney General (1981) 1 C.L.R. 543 (CA)*[228] to the effect that the interpretation of law is the exclusive province of the Judiciary. The following extract from one of the judgments[229] in *Diagoras Development* (supra) highlights the place of the doctrine of separation of powers in the constitutional order of Cyprus:

> As it is to be derived from the respective provisions of Parts IV, IX and X of our Constitution, there exists constitutionally entrenched Separation of Powers between the Legislative Power and the Judicial Power in our Republic; and the separation of the two Powers in question has been stressed in, inter alia, the judgment of Pikis J. in *Malachtou v. Attorney General of the Republic (1981) 1 C.L.R. 543, 549*, the contents of which are adopted to the extent to which this is necessary for the purposes of the present judgment.

An extract from another judgment[230] in the same case is revealing with regard to the implications of the doctrine of separation of powers:

> Subject to reservations expressly made in the Constitution (see Art. 152) every aspect of the judicial power vests in the Courts established under the Constitution. No authority other than the Judiciary can legitimately assume the exercise of any facet of the judicial power. State powers are, under the Cyprus Constitution, distributed depending on their intrinsic nature, among the three branches of the State, the Executive, the Legislative and the Judicial. Within its sphere each power is sovereign and autonomous.

*14* The ascertainment and determination in face of conflict of the facts relevant to the disposition of a judicial cause are in the province of the Judiciary. In *Papadopoulou a.o. v. Rapti a.o. (1996) 1 C.L.R. 1306 (CA)*[231] a law rendering the certification of facts by the director of the Department of Country Planning, in relation to the character of buildings, binding upon the Judiciary, was declared unconstitutional on account of

a) violation of the principle of separation of powers, and
b) breach of Article 30.2.

[228] Judgment delivered by Pikis J.
[229] That of Triantafyllides P. at page 588.
[230] That of Pikis J. at page 601.
[231] Judgment delivered by Pikis P.

The Court pronounced that the Judiciary has sole authority for the ascertainment and determination of the facts relevant to the exercise of judicial power.

The determination of the civil rights and obligations of persons and any criminal charge against them by a competent court of law through a fair trial is guaranteed as a fundamental right of the individual. No one other than the Judiciary can bring judgment to bear on the ascertainment and determination of the rights or liabilities of a person under the law. The case of *Kyriakides a.o. v. Republic (1997) 3 C.L.R. 485 (FB)*[232] is to the point. The Supreme Court declared the dismissal by the Council of Ministers of three police officers unconstitutional and for that reason void on the ground, inter alia, that the decision was premised upon the findings of a Commission of Inquiry holding the dismissed officers liable for crimes involving violations of the human rights of detainees in police custody. The Council of Ministers acted upon the finding of the aforesaid Commission to the effect that the three officers were responsible for the commission of criminal offences. Their dismissal was founded on that assumption. The Court declared the attribution of liability for the commission of a crime by anyone other than the Judiciary to be unconstitutional. The Commission of Inquiry was not a court of law. In taking its decision, the Council of Ministers overlooked or disregarded the fact that two of the three dismissed officers were tried and acquitted of the crimes ascribed to them by the Commission of Inquiry. The misdemeanour of the third officer lay in failure to exercise proper supervision over his subordinates, the other two dismissed officers, a failure that allowed them to commit the crimes imputed to them. Not only is it impermissible, the Court underlined, for anyone to attribute the commission of a crime to an individual but it is likewise forbidden to public authorities to voice suspicion against a person for the commission of a crime for which he/she was tried and acquitted.

Like principles apply in relation to disciplinary offences. Conviction for a disciplinary offence is only possible by a decision of a competent disciplinary body. In such proceedings, as often proclaimed, the person disciplinarily prosecuted is entitled to the rights assured to an accused person in criminal proceedings (Article 12.5).[233] The stringency with which denial of

232 Judgment delivered by Pikis P.

233 See inter alia Haros v. Republic 5 R.S.C.C. 39; Morsis v. Republic 4 R.S.C.C. 133; Papacleovoulou v. Republic (1982) 3 C.L.R. 187; Matsas v. Republic (1988) 3 C.L.R. 1448; Vasiliou v. Municipality of Paralimni (1996) 4 C.L.R. 1393.

the rights of the accused in disciplinary proceedings is viewed is evident from the decision in *Philippou v. Disciplinary Council (2000) 1 C.L.R. 1839 (CA)*.[234] Following the conviction of an advocate for conduct leading to his bankruptcy by the Disciplinary Council, his licence to practise was suspended for a certain period of time. Thereafter, the Council without more ado extended his suspension until reinstatement. The suspension was voided for breach of the rights of the accused under Article 12.5 (absence of charge and adequate opportunity to defend himself). Moreover, the new punishment contravened the principle embodied in Article 12.2 prohibiting the prosecution of a person twice for the same offence.

In an earlier decision, *Papageorghiou a.o. v. Republic (1990) 3 C.L.R. 1254 (FB)*,[235] the Court decided that it would be contrary to every norm of natural or administrative justice for any public authority, be it the Council of Ministers, to take disciplinary measures against officers or employees of the public, the police in that case, outside and independently of disciplinary proceedings before the competent organ of the Administration.

*15* The punishment of crime is the exclusive province of the Judiciary, as often proclaimed by the Supreme Court. In *Demetrakis Hadjisavva (1992) 1 C.L.R. 1134 (SJ)*[236] the Court re-iterated[237] that no one other than a court of law has a say in the punishment of crime and in case of imprisonment the length of it. Therefore, the application of the petitioner, a person sentenced to life imprisonment, for habeas corpus seeking his release from prison after serving a period of time in detention, based on the Prison Regulations envisaging reduction of a sentence of imprisonment[238] for specified grounds (good conduct, hard work), was rejected. Be it noted that the aforementioned Regulations were in force prior to independence and had for that reason to be applied subject to the Constitution. Only the President of the Republic on the recommendation of the Attorney-General is vested with authority to commute a sentence of imprisonment pursuant to powers specifically given to the holder of the office under Article 53.4.

In the case of *Republic v. Sampson (1991) 1 C.L.R. 858 (FB)*[239] it was decided that the relevant part of the Prisons Law CAP 286 and Regulations

[234] Judgment delivered by Pikis P.

[235] Judgment delivered by Artemides J.

[236] Judgment delivered by Pikis J.

[237] See inter alia The District Officer, Nicosia v. Georghios HajiYannis 1 R.S.C.C. 79.

[238] Sentence of life imprisonment was equated to a sentence of detention for 20 years.

[239] Judgment delivered by Pikis J.

made thereunder, in force at the time of independence, providing for the commutation of a sentence of imprisonment for good conduct, did not survive the Constitution because of its incompatibility with the principle of separation of powers requiring that punishment of crime should lie exclusively with the Judiciary.

A question that has given rise to conflicting decisions concerns the Customs 16
and Excise Law (L-82/67) specifically the constitutionality of Section 39(b) thereto empowering customs authorities to seize goods judged to have been illegally imported with a view to forfeiture. In the case *Chrysostomou v. Republic (1986) 3 C.L.R. 2666 (SJ)*[240] periodicals were seized at the port of entry on the ground that they constituted obscene publications the importation and possession of which is prohibited by the Obscene Publications Law L-35/63 on pain of punishment rendering the offender liable to imprisonment for up to two years. The Court adjudged the law to be unconstitutional for breach of:

a) the principle of separation of powers inasmuch as the decision to forfeit the articles presupposed a finding that a crime had been committed, made by a body other than a court of law;
b) the provision of Article 30.1 prohibiting extrajudicial adjudication; and
c) Article 30.2 making the determination of any criminal charge against a person the sole responsibility of a court of law.

The following passage from the judgment of the Court puts the matter in perspective: "The function of deciding whether an offence has been committed is intrinsically of a judicial character. Likewise, forfeiture as an incident of breach of penal legislation is of its nature a judicial matter".

The Court departed from the earlier decision of *Istanbouli Brothers v. The Director of Department of Customs & Excise (1986) 1 C.L.R. 465 (CA)*[241] holding that forfeiture at the instance of the Customs authorities is an administrative and not a penal measure and on that account ruled that the provisions of Article 12.3, casting the punishment of crime exclusively in the hands of the Judiciary, had no application. In not following the decision in *Istanbouli Brothers* (supra), the Court drew support from earlier authority

240 Judgment delivered by Pikis J.
241 Judgment delivered by Triantafyllides P.

*Raftis & Co v. Municipality of Paphos (1982) 2 C.L.R. 1 (CA)*[242] where punishment is depicted as "the sanction for transgressing the law" and its order has the effect " … of depriving, in one or more respects the fundamental rights of the accused, such as the right of freedom of movement and association and the rights to ownership and possession". Another decision fortifying the Court in its approach was *Zavos v. The Police (1963) 1 C.L.R. 57 (CA)*,[243] where it was determined that forfeiture, of antiquities in that case, constitutes a penal measure; hence statutory provisions for its compulsory imposition by a criminal court could not be reconciled with Article 12.3[244] that leaves punishment in the discretion of the court. Subject to certain exceptions authorized by the Constitution mandatory sentences are disallowed.[245]

The approach in *Chrysostomou* (supra) found no favour with the full bench of the Supreme Court in *Republic v. Demand Ship Co. Ltd. (1994) 3 C.L.R. 460 (FB) (majority judgment)*,[246] where it was held following *Istanbouli Brothers* (supra) that administrative fines or forfeitures are distinguishable from penalties imposed by a criminal court. Administrative sanctions have as their object the effective application of the law not the punishment of the culprit. The sanctions are limited to fines or forfeiture. A person aggrieved by a decision of the Customs Authority involving the imposition of a fine or the forfeiture of goods can have recourse to the Supreme Court under Article 146. This case was followed in the subsequent decision of *Sigma Radio TV Ltd. v. A Radio and Television Authority a.o. (2004) 3 C.L.R. 134 (P) (majority decision)*.[247]

The principle that emerges from the case law is that administrative fines and related sanctions have as sole purpose the due and efficient administration

---

[242] Concurring judgments delivered by Justices Stylianides, Loris, and Pikis.

[243] Judgments delivered by Justices Vassiliades and Josephides.

[244] It reads: No law shall provide for a punishment which is disproportionate to the gravity of the offence.

[245] Article 7.2 authorizes the imposition of the death penalty for specified offences (premeditated murder, high treason, piracy jure gentium and capital offences under military criminal law. It may be noted that the imposition of the death penalty for premeditated murder was abolished by law L86/83 substituting life imprisonment as a mandatory sentence for the death sentence. In Politis v. The Republic (1987) 2 C.L.R. 116 the Court held that provision for a mandatory sentence in this connection was in line with the spirit of the Constitution.

[246] Majority judgment delivered by Stylianides P., minority judgment delivered by Constantinides J.

[247] Majority judgment delivered by Nicolaou J.; minority judgment delivered by Nicolaides J.

of the law, as opposed to criminal proceedings determinative of the criminal responsibility of a person where sanctions involve punishment of the individual in the interests of the community and of the universal aims of law enforcement. To my mind, the distinction made is debatable and cannot be readily reconciled with the principle of separation of powers.

The distinction between administrative and criminal proceedings was the subject of comment and analysis in *Frangos v. Medical Disciplinary Board (1983) 1 C.L.R. 256 (FB)*.[248] The question the Court was required to address was the character of the Medical Council acting as a disciplinary body with authority to impose sanctions upon doctors for breaches of the Code of Ethics of the medical profession. The applicant argued that in the exercise of its disciplinary jurisdiction the Medical Council qualified as a judicial body and for that reason was liable to the supervisory power of the Supreme Court to review through certiorari and prohibition the propriety of its proceedings. The Supreme Court upholding the trial court[249] rejected the assimilation of the Medical Council to a judicial body. After review of Cyprus and English case law the Court concluded that the dominant characteristics of a judicial decision are: "a) it [the decision] must emanate out of a court of judicature and b) the decision must aim at defining the rights of the parties under the general law". 17

A similar question raised with regard to the status of the Disciplinary Board of the National Guard was likewise answered in *Christodoulou v. Disciplinary Board (1983) 1 C.L.R. 999 (FB)*.[250] In the last two decisions, the Court welcomed as salutary the fact that the provisions of Article 12.5 assuring rights to the accused in a criminal trial find application in disciplinary proceedings.

It must be clarified that the same conduct may amount to a criminal as well as a disciplinary offence. Conviction by a criminal court may in itself have implications on the status or position of a member of the public service.[251] The distinction between criminal and disciplinary proceedings was the subject of a detailed analysis in *Christodoulou v. Disciplinary Board* (supra). Disciplinary proceedings are not meant to elicit or determine either the civil rights or obligations of a person or a criminal charge against the individual.

---

[248] Judgment delivered by Pikis J.
[249] Judgment delivered by Triantafyllides P.
[250] Judgment delivered by Pikis J.
[251] Solomou v. Republic (1984) 3 C.L.R. 533.

They are intended to promote administrative ends including the efficacy, efficiency and discipline in the public service.

18 The Judiciary must more than the other two branches of the State heed the limitations of its powers. It is the only power whose acts are not liable to constitutional control by another power of the State. Furthermore, the Judiciary must not allow the judicial process to be used for any purpose other than the one for which recourse to the court is assured, notably the use of the judicial process for the resolution of disputes, identification of rights, obligations and liability for the commission of a criminal offence.

If the process of the court is abused by a litigant, the court has power to stop or suspend the proceedings. In *Director of Prisons v. Djenaro Perella (1995) 1 C.L.R. 217 (FB)*[252] the court expatiated on the nature of its inherent powers to stay proceedings involving abuse of process. No more than one proceeding may be employed for raising an issue before the court for adjudication; nor is it permissible to have recourse to the court for securing an advantage, collateral to extant proceedings. The judicial process cannot be employed in a manner oppressive to the rights of the counterparty or adversary. In the above case, the initiation of proceedings for the extradition of the respondent while proceedings for the same purpose were extant before another District Court was held to constitute an abuse of process and for that reason they were stayed.

The Court will not assume jurisdiction where it has none – *re Hadjicosta (1984) 1 C.L.R. 513 (SJ)*[253]. Recourse to the Court, on the other hand, must never draw adverse consequences for the pursuer. Access to the Court is a fundamental right assured to every person guaranteed by Article 30.1 to be protected at all times and in all circumstances (see *Theocharides v. Republic (1985) 3 C.L.R. 2725 (SJ)*[254]).

The power to punish for contempt of court is another incident of the judicial power. Such power inheres in a court of law (other than a court exercising revisional jurisdiction as earlier explained) and is entrenched by Article 162. The power is instrumental in the sustenance of the efficacy of the judicial process.[255]

The due and proper constitution of a court is a prerequisite for the assumption and exercise of judicial power. In *Mikrou v. Constantinidou (1990) 1*

---

252 Judgment delivered by Pikis J.

253 Judgment delivered by Pikis J.

254 Judgment delivered by Pikis J.

255 see Nishiotou v. Republic (1983) 3 C.L.R. 1498.

*C.L.R. 1995 (FB)*[256] the Court pronounced that an ill-constituted court lacks jurisdiction to determine a judicial cause or a matter pending before it.

The source and nature of the jurisdiction of the Supreme Court was extensively debated in a series of decisions.[257] In *Attorney General v. Artemiou (1991) 2 C.L.R. 150 (FB)*[258] and *Orphanides a.o. v. Republic (1992) 3 C.L.R. 44 (FB)*[259] it was made clear that the competence, jurisdiction and powers of the Supreme Court, established in the necessitous circumstances of Cyprus to carry out the mandate of the two superior courts derive exclusively from the Constitution and their exercise is subject to its provisions. *19*

Jurisdiction vested in the Supreme Court cannot be assigned by law to any subordinate court. For this reason in *President of the Republic v. House of Representatives (1996) 3 C.L.R. 468 (P)*[260] Section 16(3)(b) of the Protection of the Secrecy of Private Communications Law of 1996 conferring power upon one subordinate court to review the propriety of an order earlier made by another court of co-ordinate jurisdiction was declared unconstitutional for breach of the provisions of paragraphs 1 and 4 of Article 155 trusting appellate jurisdiction and jurisdiction to review the legality of a decision of an inferior court exclusively to the Supreme Court. By the impugned law power was conferred upon the Assize Court to review, in the context of criminal proceedings, an earlier order made by a judge of the District Court for the arrest of the accused and the search of the person's premises.

After the commencement of the hearing, no change in the composition of a court is permissible. If for any reason the continuation of a case before the same bench is not possible, the case must be heard anew by another judge or bench of judges as decided in *Antoniou & Sons v. Nicosia Municipality (1988) 3 C.L.R. 2495 (SJ)*.[261] The Court stressed that the hearing of a case by the same bench is a sine qua non for a valid judicial determination. The reasons warranting this course are not hard to understand or far to trace. Direct knowledge of every part and aspect of the case is essential for its appraisal. Evaluation of the evidence adduced at the trial requires a vivid pic- *20*

[256] Judgment delivered by Pikis J.

[257] President of the Republic v. House of Representative (1988) 3 C.L.R. 150; President of the Republic v. House of Representatives (No. 1) (1989) 3 C.L.R. 1490 (P); Athinis v. Republic (1989) 2 C.L.R. 71 (FB).

[258] Judgment delivered by Pikis J.

[259] Judgment delivered by Pikis J.

[260] Judgment delivered by Pikis P.

[261] Judgment delivered by Pikis J.

ture of it. The hearing of a case (the parameters of which were earlier defined) is a singular and indivisible process having from beginning to end the same purpose: to bring judgment to bear on the issues raised. In the aforementioned case, the Court signified that attaching binding force to decisions taken in the process by the judge who dealt with part of a case would interfere with the freedom of thought and conscience of the judge or bench who heard the case afresh. Such freedom inheres in every judgment maker who assumes responsibility for the determination of a case. The reasoning of a decision, an attribute of a fair trial under Article 30.2, is a composite process entailing explanation of the foundations of a judgment and the logic behind the conclusions of the Court. The right of a litigant too to present his case before the court requires that the case be heard by a court having the same composition throughout the proceedings. For similar reasons, it is impermissible for sentence to be imposed by a Judge other than the one who tried the case (see *K. Andreou Developers Ltd. v. Terlidou (2001) 2 C.L.R. 636 (CA).*[262]

*21* No cause extraneous to the ends of justice can be allowed to interrupt the hearing of judicial cases or bring the court to a standstill. So, in *Rousos a.o. v. Republic (1984) 3 C.L.R. 1437 (SJ)*[263] the Court ruled that strike action by lawyers protesting against a circular of the Supreme Court that trial courts should transact no judicial business in the chambers of Judges was found to be such an extraneous factor with the Court refusing to allow the adjournment of the hearing of a case. The above decision as well as a subsequent one on the same lines[264] were contested on appeal. The outcome was not decisive as to the acceptability of the principle espoused at first instance. The appeals were dismissed for the reason that the appropriate process for seeking the restoration of a case dismissed for want of prosecution is by way of application for reinstatement before the same court and not through an appeal (see *Rousos a.o. v. Republic (1985) 3 C.L.R. 119 (FB)*[265]). The reasoning of the first instance judgment rejecting strike action as a valid reason for the interruption of the judicial process may be traced in the following passages from its judgment:

> Judges are dutybound to administer justice according to law. In exercise of this power they are the mouthpiece of the law itself. It is the responsibility of Judges

[262] Judgment delivered by Gavrielides J.
[263] Judgment delivered by Pikis J.
[264] Theodossidaou a.o. v. Republic (1985) 3 C.L.R. 178.
[265] Judgment delivered by Triantafyllides P.

> to uphold the judicial process not only for the protection of the rights of individual litigants but also those of the public in the due administration of the law. For, it is through the efficacy of the judicial process that the rule of law can be sustained.[266]
>
> The unimpeded administration of justice is the pillar of constitutional order, and the basic safeguard for the protection of human rights, including the right of access to the Court of law. The machinery of the law cannot be allowed or suffered to come to a halt for any reason.[267]
>
> No consideration can prevail over the discharge of this duty. Judges cannot abdicate their solemn responsibility to sustain the judicial process and strive to ensure that the stream of justice flows perennially.[268]
>
> At the root of the matter is whether extra judicial causes, that is, causes unconnected with the merits of the case, are relevant and can be taken into consideration in the administration of justice.[269]
>
> Reasons of personal sensitivity have tempted me to let the matter pass and refrain from exploring the issue at depth. But my duty to administer justice according to law, allowed me no such option. Before the discharge of this duty, all my hesitations subsided, as they should. Having duly reflected on the matter before me, I find the absence of counsel and the applicant inexcusable and, on account of that reason, the recourse of the applicant liable to be dismissed. And I order its dismissal.[270]

Criminal attacks against Judges have been a rare phenomenon in Cyprus. The case of *Onoufriou v. Republic (2000) 2 C.L.R. 560 (CA)*[271] provides an exception. A litigant in civil proceedings perceiving the Judge to be inclined to decide the case against him made an attempt against his life by placing a bomb under his car designed to detonate with the ignition of the engine. The attempt was partly successful. The Judge escaped the worst but he was badly injured. The accused was found guilty of attempted murder and sentenced to 18 years imprisonment. His appeal against conviction and sentence was dismissed. Addressing the implications of the action of the accused, the Supreme Court declared on appeal that by his deeds the

266 Rousos a.o. v. Republic (1984) 3 C.L.R. 1440.

267 Rousos a.o. v. Republic (1984) 3 C.L.R. 1441.

268 Rousos a.o. v. Republic (1984) 3 C.L.R. 1441.

269 Rousos a.o. v. Republic (1984) 3 C.L.R. 1442.

270 Rousos a.o. v. Republic (1984) 3 C.L.R. 1442.

271 Judgment delivered by Pikis P.

accused "dynamited the foundation of justice, the fibre that binds society together, the nucleus of social organization".[272]

## V. The Domain of the Legislative and Executive Powers

22 The demarcation of the domain of each of the two political powers of the State under the Cyprus Constitution has been the subject of many judicial decisions. The Legislature makes the law establishing thereby the rules of governance of the country but cannot itself rule under the umbrella of legislation. Ruling under the law is the province of the Executive. Neither of the two powers can overstep the limits of its authority under the Constitution. Encroachment by one power upon the authority of the other or the judicial power will be disallowed as unconstitutional.

In *President of the Republic v. House of Representatives (1985) 3 C.L.R. 1429 (P)*[273] and *President of Republic v. House of Representatives (1985) 3 C.L.R. 1501 (P)*[274] the Supreme Court held that a decision of the House of Representatives submitted for promulgation requiring the President of the Republic to resign before the end of his term, precipitating thereby a by-election – disputed by the President as unconstitutional – was not acceptable for promulgation. The majority took the view that the decision constituted an expression of political will in relation to the Cyprus problem, a subject outside the sphere of constitutional order; therefore the decision had no constitutional foundation and for that reason could not be promulgated; it could not pass into the realm of law. The minority took the view that:

a) The decision was taken by the House of Representatives and was as such under the plain terms of Article 52 the subject of promulgation. No distinction is made between the various species of decisions for purposes of promulgation.
b) The decision was manifestly unconstitutional because of violation of the provisions of i) Article 43, specifying a five-year term in office for the President of the Republic ii) the equally clear provisions of Article 44 exhaustively enumerating the circumstances under which the office of the President could become vacant.

---

[272] Translation from Greek.

[273] Majority reasoning by Triantafyllides P., minority reasoning by Pikis J.

[274] Majority reasoning by Triantafyllides P., minority reasoning by Pikis J.

c) The decision constituted a violation of the principle of separation of powers as it involved the assumption of power by the Legislature to regulate the tenure in office of the President. The terms of office of both the President and the members of House of Representatives are laid down in the Constitution. Resignation from the office of the President is exclusively a matter for the incumbent.

Notwithstanding the disagreement among Judges concerning the non-publishability of the decision, their conclusion was the same; the decision could not be promulgated.

The sphere of authority of the two powers came under review in *President* 23
*of the Republic v. House of Representatives (1985) 3 C.L.R. 2138 (P)*[275] in a matter affecting the employment of temporary personnel. The Court held that, whereas the budget including its provisions concerning the employment of personnel is subject to legislative approval, the execution of the budget lies exclusively with the Minister of Finance as laid down in the Constitution.

The Legislature cannot through the law-making process involve itself directly or indirectly in the appointment or the termination of the services of public service personnel. The decision in *Christoudhia v. Republic (1988) 3 C.L.R. 515 (SJ)*[276] illuminates the subject. At issue was the constitutionality of law L-160/85 contested on the ground that the Legislature had overstepped the limits of its authority by providing for the permanent appointment to organic posts in the public service of personnel serving on a temporary basis; a law enacted, it must be said, with the concurrence of the Executive. The Court ruled that the appointment of members of the public service was exclusively an administrative matter outside the sphere of the Legislature. By assuming power to effect the appointment of public employees, the Legislature stepped into the province of the Executive. By the same process they sought to prescribe the relevant schemes of service regulating the qualification for appointment to the public service, a matter again within the sphere of the Executive.[277] Moreover, the House of Representatives, a political body, immersed itself in the process of appointment of civil servants, contrary to the principle, earlier explained, of separation between political and administrative authorities. Lastly, they usurped the powers of

---

275 Judgment delivered by Triantafyllides P.

276 Judgment delivered by Pikis J.

277 President of the Republic v. House of Representatives (1985) 3 C.L.R. 1724.

the Public Service Commission the sole authority responsible for the selection and appointment of personnel in the public service.

On appeal, the judgment was reversed mainly on grounds of social necessity citing the concurrence of the two political powers of the State as declaratory of the necessity arising to settle the problem (see *Republic v. Christoudhia (1988) 3 C.L.R. 2622 (FB) (majority decision)*[278]). The minority held that benevolent as the motives of the Legislature in enacting the law may have been, no justification could be found for the assumption of power beyond the range of its authority. The majority too was not oblivious to the implications of legislative action indicating that law L-160/85 was not a precedent to be repeated. Years later, the decision on appeal in *Christoudhia* (supra) was held to be ill-founded and for that reason it was not followed. Occasion for review of this judicial precedent presented itself in *Republic v. Yiallourou (1995) 3 C.L.R. 363 (FB)*,[279] where a similar question arose concerning the constitutionality of a law (L-164/90) prescribing the appointment of temporary government personnel while limiting the competence of the Public Service Commission to rubber stamping the appointment of the defined class of persons. Amenity to depart from judicial precedent, the Court explained, is acknowledged whenever the principle upon which it rests is manifestly ill-founded. In addition to breaching the principle of separation of powers and constitutional provisions relevant to the appointment of public service personnel, the impugned law violated, the Court found, the principle of equality of treatment of persons in the same position (Article 28) binding upon all powers of the State and assuring an equal right to everybody having the qualifications to compete for appointment to a position in the public service.

The problem of incorporating temporary personnel as permanent members of the public service by unorthodox means was a recurrent one. Many attempts were made to achieve this goal through the legislative process but with no success. The decisions in *Menelaou a.o. v. Republic a.o. (1996) 3 C.L.R. 370 (FB)*[280] and *Elia a.o. v. Republic (1999) 3 C.L.R. 884 (FB)*[281] closed the door to any further attempts to bypass through legislation the constitutional process for the appointment of personnel in the public service.

[278] Majority judgment delivered by Stylianides J., minority judgment delivered by A. Loizou P.
[279] Judgment delivered by Pikis J.
[280] Judgment delivered by Pikis P.
[281] Judgment delivered by Pikis P.

The Court reiterated that the Public Service Commission is the only authority with power to make appointments to positions in the public service. Its discretion as to who should be selected should not be fettered by any constraints whatsoever. Every vacancy must be advertised assuring thereby the right of everyone having the qualifications to apply for appointment. The right of equality of opportunity legitimises every prospective candidate to seek the review of decisions made outside the ordained process. In the case of *Elia* (supra) the Court stressed that personalised legislation and incorporation therein of administrative decisions offend the principle of equality assured in all respects by Article 28 (see also *Georghiou a.o. v. Republic (1997) 3 C.L.R. 81 (FB)*[282]).

From the early days of the Republic it was acknowledged that not only executive power specifically assigned to organs of the Executive by the Constitution 24
but the residue (unallocated executive power) of executive authority also vests in the Executive; in particular in its principal organ, the Council of Ministers (see *Theodoros G. Papapetrou v. Republic 2 R.S.C.C. 61*[283]).

The case of *President of the Republic v. House of Representatives (1985) 3 C.L.R. 2165 (P)*[284] enlightens about the distribution of State power between the Executive and the Legislature. Upon the dissolution of the Greek Communal Chamber by a vote of the Chamber itself, need arose in the necessitous circumstances that followed to allocate its power to the authority of the State to which the intrinsic nature of such power predestined it. The Communal Chamber was vested with both executive and legislative power in the area of its competence. Law L-12/65 sought to distribute the powers of the Communal Chamber between the legislative and the executive branches of government according to its juridical characteristics. At issue was the propriety of the division of power effected between the Legislature and the Executive. The Court found the law to be in line with the principle of separation of powers inasmuch as the legislative authority of the Communal Chamber was transferred to the House of Representatives and its executive power, including the appointment of teaching personnel, was assigned to authorities of the Executive, notably the Ministry of Education and the Educational Service Commission, the body trusted with authority to make appointments and promotions of teachers and exercise disciplinary jurisdiction over them.

282 Judgment delivered by Pikis P.

283 The judgment of the Court was read by Forsthoff P.

284 Judgments delivered by Triantafyllides P. and Pikis J.

Two other cases demonstrate the absoluteness of the rule that the Legislature should refrain from treading into the field of the Executive. These are *President of the Republic v. House of Representatives (No. 1) (2000) 3 C.L.R. 157 (P)*[285] and *President of the Republic v. House of Representatives (No. 1) (2001) 3 C.L.R. 83 (P)*[286]. In the first reference at issue was the constitutionality of a distinct provision of a law for the recognition of the struggles of Cypriots for freedom and liberty. The task of recognition of individual contribution was assigned to a Committee whose members would be selected by the Executive subject to confirmation by the House of Representatives. In the second case, at issue was the constitutionality of a Committee envisaged by law for the recognition of the struggles of Cypriots to resist the coup d'état of 15th July 1974 that toppled the democratically elected government of the country. The members of the Committee would be appointed by the Executive with the concurrence of the House of Representatives. In both cases the relevant provisions of the law affecting participation of the Legislature in the appointment of the members of the administrative bodies in question were found to be unconstitutional. In no circumstances can the involvement of the Legislature in the administrative process be justified. As the offensive provisions were severable from the remaining parts of the two laws, only those segments of the enactments were disclaimed.

*25* The case of *President of the Republic v. House of Representatives (1994) 3 C.L.R. 93 (P) (majority decision)*[287] seeks to earmark the frontiers of the executive and legislative powers. A reference to the background of the issues posed for judicial consideration is essential for understanding the decision in its proper perspective. In the year 1980, the Council of Ministers, in exercise of powers vested in it by law (L-57/78), dismissed 62 persons holding positions in public services on grounds of complicity or support of the coup d'état. In 1993 the Council of Ministers appointed by a new President of the Republic recalled the previous decisions ex nunc paving the way for the return of the dismissed persons to various branches of public services, including the National Guard and the Police Force. The House of Representatives reacted negatively to this decision and adopted a number of measures aimed to frustrate it. Firstly, a decision was taken calling upon the

[285] Judgment delivered by Pikis P.

[286] Judgment delivered by Pikis P.

[287] Majority judgment delivered by Pikis J, minority judgment delivered by A. Loizou P.

Council of Ministers in mandatory terms to revoke the decision made. Secondly, through an amendment of the budget, a legislative measure, they sought to make reemployment of the dismissed persons impossible. Thirdly, the budget law was amended in a manner designed to eliminate the possibility of funds being allocated for the reemployment of the dismissed officers. Fourthly, a law was introduced amending the pension law to the effect that persons reemployed in the public service would not earn any pension rights for the period that they were absent from their duties. The following decisions were taken by the Court (majority decisions):

a) The decision of the House of Representatives requiring the Council of Ministers to revoke its decision was a proper subject for promulgation and in consequence its constitutionality could be reviewed under the provisions of Article 140. The decision was adjudged to be unconstitutional because the revocation of a decision of the Executive was a matter exclusively within the domain of the Executive. One power of the state, it was said, cannot dictate to another power the decisions it ought to take or the manner in which it should exercise its powers.
b) The law amending the budget in a way designed to frustrate the decision was manifestly unconstitutional for breach of the principle of separation of powers. The House of Representatives exceeded its powers in that it legislated in order to annul an administrative decision. This was a classical example of personalized legislation designed to administer through the law.
c) The amendment of the budget making the allocation of funds dependent on who should hold positions in the public service was likewise unconstitutional for stepping into the domain of the Administration and using the law as an instrument of executive power.
d) The amendment of the Pensions Law, whereby persons like the reinstated officers staying out of the service would not be entitled in the event of re-employment to pension rights for the period of their absence, was not unconstitutional. The law established a legal norm applicable to everyone in a matter properly within the sphere of the Legislature.

The minority took the view that:

a) The decision of the House of Representatives could not be the subject of promulgation, for that reason no issue could be raised respecting its constitutionality.

b) The amendment of the budget did not involve any increase of expenditure. Hence, the House of Representatives could write off expenditures necessary for the re-employment of the dismissed officers.

26 An attempt by the House of Representatives to reverse through legislation administrative action was likewise turned down as unconstitutional in *Michael Theodosiou Ltd. v. Municipality of Limassol (1993) 3 C.L.R. 25 (FB)*.[288] The law, the constitutionality of which came up for consideration, envisaged the repeal of an order of acquisition of immovable property. The Court held that the subject of legislation was a purely administrative measure outside the powers and beyond the authority of the Legislature.

The Constitution specifies the Ministries to be ten in number. The self-dissolution of the Greek Communal Chamber was found, as earlier indicated, in *President of the Republic v. House of Representatives (1985) 3 C.L.R. 2801 (P)*[289] to justify the establishment of a Ministry of Education to take over its administrative competencies. The establishment of Ministries is exclusively within the power of the President of the Republic in virtue of Article 46, subject to constitutional limitations as to their number. Consequently, a law specifying the Ministries of the State was held to be unconstitutional. On the other hand, the assignment of duties and responsibilities to the various Ministries of the State is in the power of the Legislature. As much was decided in *President of the Republic v. House of Representatives (1985) 3 C.L.R. 2779 (P)*.[290]

27 Governmental action in the exercise of executive power of the State is, as already explained, subject to judicial review under Article 146. The exercise of such power is subject to the fetters of the law including the norms of due and proper administration (sound administration) implicit in the exercise of executive and administrative authority. Characteristic of these constraints is the case of *Antoniades a.o. v. Republic (1997) 3 C.L.R. 295 (FB)*.[291] The Court was required to determine the validity of a decision of the Council of Ministers to terminate the services of members of the Board of the Electricity Authority, a public corporation, pending an inquiry into the circumstances surrounding the award of a tender for the supply of services to the Authority. The termination of the services of the members of the

[288] Judgment delivered by Pikis J.

[289] Judgment delivered by Triantafyllides P.

[290] Judgment delivered by Triantafyllides P.

[291] Judgment delivered by Pikis P.

Board of the Electricity Authority was made in the interest of the efficacy of the inquiry. The decision was annulled on the ground that appointments made by the Executive cannot be terminated at will but only in the presence of valid reasons establishing deviation on the part of members from the due exercise of their duties. Such a shortfall is noticeable whenever it is made to appear that they exercise their powers not in a manner promoting the objects of the law, they are trusted to administer, but for extraneous purposes; a principle identified in the earlier case of *Stephanides a.o. v. Republic (1993) 3 C.L.R. 367 (FB)*,[292] where the Court stressed that public interest is not a panacea. Public interest is inseverable from the ends of the law by reference to which it is defined. Public interest is not tied to the perception of a government as to what is good and expedient in any given situation but with the promotion of the objects of the law.

*Makrides a.o. v. Republic (1984) 3 C.L.R. 677 (SJ)*[293] underlines that power conferred upon a specific organ cannot be exercised by another organ of the Executive. Thus, an appointment made by the Council of Ministers to the position of Registration Officer was annulled for the reason that sole authority for making appointments in the public service vested with the Public Service Commission. *28*

In making the law as well as in administering it, the Legislature and the Executive must heed the principle of equality in all its manifestations, a sine qua non for the validity of every action.[294]

With the exception of taxation and the imposition of duties or rates, the Constitution does not prohibit retrospective legislation. Nevertheless, such species of legislation is generally unwelcome. It upsets certainty in the law, vital for its efficacy. The Interpretation Law CAP 1 provides that legislation should be construed prospectively unless there is a clear indication to the contrary in the statute itself (see Section 10). The Constitution does not prohibit retrospective legislation except with regard to the imposition of taxes, duties and rates of any kind. In *Papanicopoulos v. Morphou Co-operative (1986) 3 C.L.R. 288 (P)*[295] the Court explained that in legislating retrospectively the Legislature must heed fundamental rights especially the right to equality. In the aforesaid case as well as in the earlier one of *Sandis v.* *29*

[292] Judgment delivered by A. Loizou P.

[293] Judgment delivered by Pikis J.

[294] See inter alia President of the Republic v. House of Representatives (1987) 3 C.L.R. 1631.

[295] Judgments delivered by Triantafyllides P., A. Loizou J., Pikis J.

*Republic (1983) 3 C.L.R. 419 (SJ)*[296] the Court took pains to explain the attributes of retrospective legislation. Changing existing law by reference to events or circumstances of the past does not make the law retroactive. Retrospective is legislation that upsets vested rights, that is rights that accrued under the law at a date prior to its promulgation by taking them away or diminishing them. Conferring rights by reference to past events does not constitute retrospective legislation. In the case of *Michael Theodosiou Ltd v. Municipality of Limassol* (supra) the Court affirmed that a law is not retroactive unless its application is extended backwards to a date prior to its promulgation. Definitive of the concept of vested rights is the decision of the Supreme Court in the case of *Republic v. Menelaou (1982) 3 C.L.R. 419 (FB).*[297]

[296] Judgment delivered by Pikis J.
[297] Judgment delivered by Pikis J.

# G

# Article 146 "Judicial Review of Administrative Action"

## I. Judicial Review of Administrative Action under the Constitution

The Constitution introduced judicial review of administrative action as a separate jurisdiction distinguishable from every other judicial process. Article 146 institutionalizes judicial review of administrative action, i.e. action emanating from the exercise of executive or administrative authority in an all-embracing manner; a jurisdiction previously unknown to Cyprus law. The jurisdiction is founded on the continental prototype making judicial review of acts of the Administration a permanent feature of the judicial system and the system of government generally; a species of jurisdiction originating from France institutionalised in Napoleonic times, in the year 1799, as a bulwark against maladministration. The jurisdiction was entrusted to the Conseil d'État, an institution separate from the conventional branches of the Judiciary. The jurisprudence of the French Council of State played a major role in the development of the principles of administrative law in the continent of Europe and beyond. In addition to its judicial authority, an advisory role was acknowledged to the French Council of State to opine on 1 the acceptability of legal instruments to be issued or made. The advisory functions of the Council cannot properly be classified as judicial. The conferment of power upon a court of law to render advice to the other powers of the State, as distinct from pronouncing on the constitutionality or legality of their acts and decisions, is antithetical to the principle of separation of powers. By confining the competence and jurisdiction of the Supreme Constitutional Court of Cyprus to judicial review of action or inaction of the Administration, the purity of the system of separation of powers is preserved as well as that of the judicial process.

In the context of Cyprus' constitutional order, judicial review became a potent instrument for the protection of the fundamental rights and liberties of man duly incorporated in the Constitution. As earlier indicated, Article 35, the last Article of the Part safeguarding human rights, imposes a direct obligation upon all authorities of the State not only to heed human rights in the exercise of their powers but to secure their "efficient application" too; casting a positive duty upon the Administration to give expression to them in its entire field of action.

*2* Judicial review of administrative action as a separate branch of substantive and procedural law was unknown to English law at the time of Cyprus' independence. Such limited amenity as was available to the ordinary courts of law to oversee the legality of the administrative process derived from jurisdiction to grant writs known as prerogative writs[296] (mandamus, certiorari, prohibition, quo warranto) primarily intended to ensure that organs of government acted in specified situations in conformity with the law and within the boundaries of their jurisdiction.

Judicial review of administrative action enriched the armoury of the law for the sustenance of the rule of law. Under colonial legislation, the legal means available for the protection of one's rights were limited to those provided for by civil and criminal law. Public law rights other than those deriving from criminal law were not acknowledged to a person except rights associated with protection against arbitrary detention for which the writ of habeas corpus was available. The effect of Article 146 was to render public law rights justiciable at the instance of a person or body whose legitimate interests were prejudicially affected by action or inaction of the Administration.

---

[296] Emanating from the Crown.

Article 146.1 vests jurisdiction to review administrative action exclusively in the Supreme Constitutional Court.[297] No other court can assume directly or indirectly jurisdiction to review acts, decisions or omissions of the Administration. To whatever extent an administrative act or decision is relevant to a judicial pronouncement in the context of civil or criminal proceedings it must be accepted and acted upon without demurral. Thus, in a prosecution of a person for failure to pay tax due, the criminal court will not inquire into the validity of the tax decision. Its jurisdiction is limited to ascertaining whether the decision was duly taken and communicated to the person affected and if so whether there was failure to comply with it. A tax decision can only be contested by a recourse raised under Article 146. In that context alone can the validity of such a decision be tested. Likewise, a person who violates the conditions of a building licence cannot impugn the validity of the licensing decision before a criminal court in a prosecution for building contrary to the conditions of the permit (see inter alia *Elia v. Improvement Board of Xylophagou (1994) 2 C.L.R. 173 (CA)*[298] and *Kyriakides a.o. v. Commissioner for Value Added Tax (1999) 2 C.L.R. 75 (CA)*[299]). The same applies to civil proceedings. In no circumstances will the court inquire into the validity of an administrative act or decision (see inter alia *Takis P. Makrides v. Attorney General (1997) 1 C.L.R. 1424 (CA)*[300] *and Philippa Estate Ltd. a.o. v. Sewage Board Limassol Amathontos (2001) 1 C.L.R. 1026 (CA)*[301]). 3

## II. Acts, Decisions and Omissions of the Administration Subject to Judicial Review

Article 146.1 reads: 4

> The Supreme Constitutional Court shall have exclusive jurisdiction to adjudicate finally on a recourse made to it on a complaint that a decision, an act or omission of any organ, authority or person, exercising any executive or administrative authority is contrary to any of the provisions of this Constitution or of any law or is made in excess or in abuse of powers vested in such organ or authority or person.

[297] Subsequently the Supreme Court.
[298] Judgment delivered by Pikis J.
[299] Judgment delivered by Pikis P.
[300] Judgment delivered by Pikis P.
[301] Judgment delivered by Pikis P.

Each one of the three descriptive terms "decision", "act" or "omission" may attract a number of kindred meanings. Every kind of resolution may be characterized as a decision and every outward manifestation of the exercise of public authority may qualify as an act. Omission again may refer to every form of inaction on the part of the Administration. The three terms "act", "decision" and "omission" attract their precise meaning from the context in which they appear. Under consideration is the review of action or inaction of the Administration at the behest of an aggrieved party. From the outset it was made clear that only acts and decisions definitive of the rights and obligations of the person affected thereby are justiciable, or omissions importing similar consequences; in other words, only action or inaction of the Administration productive of legal consequences can be the subject of review. Such an act or decision of the Administration is characterized as executory.

5 In *Stephanides v. Municipality of Engomi (1994) 3 C.L.R. 49 (FB)*[302] the Court summed up the principles surrounding the emergence of an executory act or decision: Executoriness connotes action expressive of the will of the Administration determinative in itself of the rights and obligations of the subject(s) of the decision. Executory acts or decisions may be contrasted to acts or decisions of the Administration of an informatory, advisory or confirmatory character. An informatory act or decision is one providing information on behalf of an administrative body, person or organ respecting its authority, competence or plans of action. An advisory act or decision of the Administration is one rendering advice to a person with regard to what is necessary or required to be done in order to achieve an administrative goal. In neither case is the act or decision conclusive about the rights or obligations of a person. A confirmatory act or decision is one affirming or reaffirming an earlier executory act or decision of the Administration signifying adherence to a course of action or stand already taken. Such decision may acquire an executory character notwithstanding its identity with an earlier one if it arises or results from an inquiry into new facts, previously unknown, relevant to the subject matter of the decision (see inter alia *Thalassinos v. Republic (1998) 3 C.L.R. 364 (FB)*[303]). A request to re-examine an executory act or decision does not cast an obligation upon the

[302] Judgment delivered by Pikis J.
[303] Judgment delivered by Nikitas J.

Administration to do so unless accompanied by the citation of or reference to new facts having a bearing on the subject matter of the decision (see inter alia *Varnava v. Republic (1968) 3 C.L.R. 566 (SJ)*[304] and *Pieris v. Republic (1983) 3 C.L.R. 1054 (FB)*[305]). The non-justiciability of confirmatory acts or decisions rules out any possibility of by-passing the strictness of the time limit set by the Constitution (Article 146.3) for mounting a recourse against reviewable acts or decisions of the Administration (Article 146.3).

An omission on the part of an organ or authority of the Administration to act in response to a request of a person to do so is not reviewable per se despite the provisions of Article 29. The omission becomes justiciable only if the request refers to the issuing of a potentially executory act or an omission the Administration is law bound to remedy.[306] Article 29.1 requires that a reasoned decision be rendered by the Administration in response to a written request or complaint of an individual within 30 days. The rendering of a reasoned decision presupposes examination of the subject matter of the request or complaint. Consequently, the law that should govern the taking of the decision should be the one in force within the 30 day period. As much was decided in the case of *Christoforou a.o. v. The Municipal Committee of Ay. Dhometios a.o. (1987) 3 C.L.R. 1464 (SJ).*[307] This view was not espoused by the plenum of the Supreme Court on appeal – *The Municipal Committee of Ay. Dhometios v. Christoforou (1994) 3 C.L.R. 434 (FB)*[308] – , where it was held that Article 29 does not override the general rule of administrative law that decisions of the Administration must be taken within a reasonable time from the moment the Administration is moved to act. Sequentially, the law applicable is that obtaining within the time span that may be objectively regarded as reasonable in the circumstances of the case. Reasonableness of time in this area is determined by the complexity of the case and the magnitude of the inquiry necessary to ascertain the facts material for the taking of the decision. It still appears to me hard to reconcile this decision with the *6*

[304] Judgment delivered by Hadjianastassiou J.

[305] Judgment delivered by Pikis J.

[306] See inter alia Xenofontos v. Republic 2 R.S.C.C. 89; Andreas Kyriakides v. C.B.C. (1965) 3 C.L.R. 746; Modestos Pitsillos v. The Minister of the Interior through the Director General a.o. (1971) 3 C.L.R. 397 and Papadopoulos v. Municipality of Nicosia (1986) 3 C.L.R. 2046.

[307] Judgment delivered by Pikis J.

[308] Judgment delivered by Stylianides P.

wording of Article 29,[309] especially with the requirement to give a reasoned decision within a fixed interval of time.

Due reasoning of an administrative act or decision is an indispensable element for its validity. Article 29 safeguards, as a fundamental right of the individual, speedy administration imposing a duty upon State authorities to address requests and complaints of a person in a manner befitting a society ordered by law. The human right to speedy administration is in many respects akin to the right that justice should be administered within a reasonable time; elicitation of rights and obligations is at issue in both cases.

*7* Save for inaction to address a request or complaint under Article 29, the implications of which were outlined above, omission as such to exercise power pertaining to the issuing of an administrative act or decision is not justiciable except with respect to acts or decisions that the Administration is legally bound to issue. A party prejudicially affected by an omission of this kind has a right to seek judicial review of the failure of the Administration to act. Where the Administration fails to carry out a duty cast upon it by law, a party prejudicially affected thereby can have recourse to the Court to review the omission. The obligation to carry out such a duty does not cease until fulfilled and time does not stop running for purposes of judicial review until the omission is remedied. Consequently, knowledge of the omission by the pursuer does not activate the time limit of 75 days for raising a recourse (see *Phylactides v. Republic (1983) 3 C.L.R. 957 (SJ)*[310]).

## III. The Public Domain

*8* Rule according to law and the exercise of the powers vested thereunder for the promotion of its ends define the mandate of public administration. The canons evolved over time defining the rules of proper or sound administration

[309] It reads: 1. Every person has the right individually or jointly with others to address written requests or complaints to any competent public authority and to have them attended to and decided expeditiously; an immediate notice of any such decision taken duly reasoned shall be given to the person making the request or complaint and in any event within a period not exceeding thirty days. 2. Where any interested person is aggrieved by any such decision or where no such decision is notified to such person within the period specified in paragraph 1 of this Article, such person may have recourse to a competent court in the matter of such request or complaint.

[310] Judgment delivered by Pikis J.

form the principles of administrative law. An act or decision of the Administration must be preceded by a due inquiry into the material facts of the case held in the context of the law applicable to the subject and supported by the reasons founding it. Thus, the decision of the Administration must be duly informed and duly reasoned.

The public domain is contrasted to the private domain of law. Public administration operates as a rule in the public domain but its competencies do not end there. The Administration is also entrusted with authority pertaining to the management of the fiscus covering every species of State property. In that area, the State is in the same position as any other owner of property. Its conduct and actions are governed by the rules of private law.

Only acts, decisions or omissions of the Administration emanating from the exercise of powers in the public domain are amenable to judicial review under Article 146.1. Administrative power in this context involves, as a rule, discretion to be exercised in a manner promoting the ends of the law. Decision making is not subject to the agreement or consent of a third party. The Administration acts unilaterally conferring thereby rights to or imposing obligations upon persons. The unilateral expression of the will of the Administration is the determinative factor for the content of the act or decision; a species of imperium. Acts or decisions of the Administration lacking this attribute and not productive of legal consequences are not amenable to judicial review. To this category belongs the provision of services by the land registry and other departments involving an act or a decision identifying a person's private law rights. In those circumstances, the acts of the Administration do not generate rights nor do they impose obligations but merely identify rights existing under the law. This point is exemplified by the case of *Antoniou a.o. v. Republic (1984) 3 C.L.R. 623 (SJ)*.[311] Under the Immovable Property (Tenure Registration and Valuation) Law CAP 224 the Director of the Lands and Surveys Department is given power to locate the boundaries of immovable property in case of doubt or a dispute between owners of adjoining land. The decision of the Director involves identification of property rights by reference to the official topographical map of the area. In the above case the Court, treading the path earmarked by earlier authority, decided that the decision of the Director in this sphere is not subject to judicial review. Such decisions are bound up with the private law rights of a person. The decision of the Director does not add or detract from

[311] Judgment delivered by Pikis J.

those rights. It merely ascertains them as reflected in their title deeds and as correlated to the topographical plan of the area (see *Republic v. Toka (1995) 3 C.L.R. 218 (FB)*[312]). There is no doubt an element of decision making in this area too, but it is a decision referable to existing rights; no rights spring therefrom. A party aggrieved by the decision of the Director may dispute it by making an appeal before a civil court trusted with jurisdiction to examine the correctness of the decision of the Director. Similarly, a decision of the Director to correct errors in the land register for which provision is also made in Section 49 of CAP 224 cannot become the subject of a recourse under Article 146.1 but – as in the case of identification of boundaries – a party who disputes the correctness of the decision may appeal to a civil court. In *Alkiviadou a.o. v. Constantinou a.o. (2001) 1 C.L.R. 2133 (CA)*[313] the Court pointed out that Section 49, making provision for registration of land, like other pre-independence legislation, must be read and applied subject to the Constitution; the relevant provisions being in this context those of Article 30.2 trusting the determination of any question affecting the civil rights and obligations of a person to a competent court established by law.[314] Property rights are per se referable to a person's civil rights as repeatedly affirmed (see inter alia *Phani v. Director of the Lands and Surveys Department (1999) 1 C.L.R. 1760 (CA)*,[315] *Apostolou v. Efhtymiou (2000) 1 C.L.R. 906 (CA)*[316].

Neither the Director nor any other administrative authority can assume power under the Immovable Property Law or any other law to determine a person's rights to property. Under Article 30.2 only a court of law has competence to determine the civil rights and obligations of a person; a category to which property rights belong. In the case of *Hassidoff v. Santi a.o. (1970) 1 C.L.R. 220 (CA)*[317] and subsequent decisions[318] it was stressed that under no guise and in no circumstances can the Director of the Lands and Surveys Department adjudicate upon or determine disputes affecting the ownership of land. In *Hassidoff* (supra) the Court held that the Director has no right

[312] Judgment delivered by Pikis P.
[313] Judgment delivered by Pikis P.
[314] See also Ibrahim Mehmed Chakkoto v. the Attorney-General (1961) C.L.R. 231.
[315] Judgment delivered by Pikis P.
[316] Judgment delivered by Pikis P.
[317] Judgment delivered by Josephides J.
[318] see inter alia Republic v. Toka (supra) and Hellenic Bank v. Republic (1986) 3 C.L.R. 481.

to determine whether land registered in the name of A became the property of B on account of adverse possession (usucapio).

The test to determine whether an act or decision is justiciable under Article 146 revolves around the primary object of the act or decision. If the decision is primarily aimed to promote a public purpose, it falls in the domain of public law. As much was decided in *Achilleas Hadjikyriacou v. Theologia Hadjiapostolou a.o. 3 R.S.C.C. 89*[319] and *Savvas Vianni Valana v. Republic 3 R.S.C.C. 91.*[320] In *Antoniou a.o. v. Republic* (supra) the Court sought to identify what a public purpose is: "A public purpose is one in which the public at large or a noticeable section of it has an interest in the sense that its proper promotion has repercussions extending beyond those immediately affecting the parties directly affected thereby." The public, it was stated, has a limited interest in the adjustment or definition of private law rights unless such determination is incidental to a wider purpose in which case judicial review is feasible. The demarcation of the public and private domain approved in *Antoniou a.o. v. Republic* (supra) was espoused in *Machlouzarides v. Republic a.o. (1985) 3 C.L.R. 2342 (FB).*[321] 9

The interest of the public in a given area of administrative action is the principal consideration for depicting the public domain. Judicial review aims to protect the public interest in areas of administrative action of concern to the public. Acts and decisions of the Administration in the public domain spring, as a rule, from the exercise of discretionary powers vested in the Administration for the due enforcement or application of the law. How these powers are exercised is of great consequence to the public. Correspondingly low is the interest of the public in the identification or adjustment of private law rights, the vestees of which have the means to protect their interests by recourse to a civil court. In *Pantelidou a.o. v. Water Board of Nicosia (1990) 3 C.L.R. 3397 (FB)*[322] the Supreme Court addressed the following question: Was a decision of the Nicosia Water Board to rescind the rights of persons who had title deeds to the supply of water by virtue of contractual obligations of the forerunners of the Water Board reviewable under Article 146? The majority gave a negative answer to the question holding that the issue arising is one affecting private law rights, 10

[319] Judgment of the Court read by Forsthoff P.

[320] Judgment of the Court read by Forsthoff P.

[321] Judgment delivered by Stylianides J.

[322] Majority judgment delivered by Stylianides J.; minority judgment delivered by Pikis J.

deriving from a contractual relationship. The minority, on the other hand, decided that the action was justiciable because the act of termination emanated from the exercise of powers given by law and not in virtue of contractual rights. The contract regulated respective rights and obligations, subject to the overriding provisions of the law as to their duration, affecting a matter of great consequence to the public, the supply of water.

*11* Public interest in the administrative process is not static. A lot depends on the repercussions of administrative action upon the general public and its corresponding interest in the subject. Judicial review is a legal process designed to uphold the interest of the public in sound administration. The point is illustrated by the case of *Republic v. M.D.M. Estate Developments Ltd. (1982) 3 C.L.R. 642 (FB) (majority judgment)*[323] where it was decided that decisions of the Lands and Surveys Department respecting the specification of the reserve price, that is the price below which immovable property under compulsory sale should not be sold, ceased to be a matter of interest to the public and on that account the decision was not subject to judicial review. They came to this decision after a survey of the social and economic realities of Cyprus. In view of the decline of public interest in the matter, judicial review ceased to offer itself as a necessary means for the protection of essentially private law rights. Unlike olden days, compulsory sales of immovable property, especially of properties in rural areas, became a rare phenomenon resulting in a sequential drop of the interest of the public in the matter. Consequently, the raison d'être for elevating decisions relevant to private law rights in the domain of public law disappeared. On that account they distinguished earlier first instance judgments[324] to the contrary.

*12* Earlier we noted that acts of the Administration referable to the fiscus are not reviewable under Article 146.1. Acts and decisions of the Administration in that area do not derive from the exercise of any kind of imperium. The Administration does not determine what is to be. On the contrary, its position and rights are defined by private law. In managing its property, the Administration is in the same position as any other person.

[323] Majority judgment delivered by Hadjianastasiou J., minority judgment delivered by Triantafyllides P.

[324] Cyprus Industrial and Mining Co Ltd (No. 1) v. The Republic (1966) 3 C.L.R. 94; Galip v. The Minister of Interior a.o. (1974) 3 C.L.R. 74.

Contracts executed on behalf of the State regarding the lease of State property or any other contractual undertaking are subject to private law. Acts of the fiscus may be preceded by decisions of the Administration taken in the domain of public law. Those decisions are justiciable. Hence, a decision of the Tender Board to award a contract for the supply of goods or services to the public to any of the tenderers is a decision subject to judicial review. The criteria, by reference to which the selection of the least costly tender is made, are a matter of vital interest to the public. The contract that is executed sequentially thereto between the Administration and the successful tenderer and the relationship between the two parties is governed by private law. Any dispute regarding the execution of the contract is subject to the jurisdiction of a civil court (see *Nautical Club Paphos v. Cyprus Ports Authority (1991) 1 C.L.R. 1147 (CA)*[325]).

Article 146.1 postulates in terms the justiciability of every executory act or decision in the domain of public law issued in the exercise of executive or administrative authority. The Court has not attempted to draw the line between executive and administrative authority or categorise acts and decisions by reference to the nature of the authority wherefrom they derive. The inclusion of acts, decisions or omissions emanating from the exercise of or failure to exercise either species of authority appears to cover the entire field of action of the Executive. The only exception to the reviewability of actions of the Executive, acknowledged by the case law, are acts known in French law as *actes de gouvernement.*[326] Justification for the exception may be found in the fact that the exercise of such power is not subject to any criteria set by law. The will of the Executive, the President or the Council of Ministers, is the determinative factor for the decision to be made. For such acts, the Executive is politically accountable. Presidential appointments of the chairman and of members of the Public Service Commission[327] and the Chief of the police and his deputy[328] as well as decisions bearing on the exercise of the prerogative of mercy[329] have been acknowledged to be *actes de gouvernement.* Moreover, it has been decided that appointments of Judges to the *13*

[325] Judgment delivered by Pikis J.

[326] The nearest to this term in English law is "acts of State".

[327] See Louca v. Republic (1983) 3 C.L.R. 783; see also Republic v. Louca a.o. (1984) 3 C.L.R. 241.

[328] See Stokkos v. The Republic (1983) 3 C.L.R. 1411.

[329] See Demetriou v. Republic 3 R.S.C.C. 121.

Supreme Court are not subject to judicial review.[330] By the same token, it may be assumed that appointments of Ministers and the appointment of the Attorney-General belong to the same category of acts. On the other hand, it has been decided that refusal of entry to the country to an alien does not qualify as an act of government but on the contrary, it is reviewable.[331] The principles relevant to this aspect of administrative law were reviewed in *Hadjiandreou v. The Republic (2001) 3 C.L.R. 352 (FB).*[332] It is noted that the case law does not provide a comprehensive definition of acts that may be thus classified. Another inference is that the Court will not readily identify acts or decisions of the Executive as forming part of this category. In *Hadjiandreou* (supra) the Court recognized the termination of the appointment of an honorary consul as an act of government. Such appointments and sequentially their termination constitute an aspect of foreign affairs (Articles 50 and 54) and as such are subject to the unfettered discretion of the Council of Ministers. Honorary consuls are not members of the public service nor is their appointment or its termination subject to any rules.

The provisions of Article 146 leave no room for exempting from judicial review any acts or decisions deriving from the exercise of executive authority. The absence of rules regulating the exercise of power is not of itself a valid reason for removing such action from reviewable acts or decisions. The Executive is bound, in that case too, to observe the norms of good administration. A possible justification is that *actes de gouvernement* are outside the normative framework of the administration and as such not amenable to review. The choice made by the executive organ as such is the determinative force for the genesis of the act. One may discern common characteristics between acts of government and acts of State under English law, a subject upon which I shall not dwell.

*14* Acts or decisions of the Executive unrelated to the promotion of the ends of the Administration as such are not amenable to judicial review. Decisions of this nature involve the exercise of authority pertaining to the other powers of the State. Their entrustment by the Constitution to the Executive constitutes a deviation from the principle of separation of powers. To this category belong decisions of the President of the Republic in the exercise of the prerogative of mercy entitling the President to remit, suspend or commute a sentence of a court of law with the concurrence of the Attorney General

[330] See Level Tachexaves Ltd (No. 1) (1995) 1 C.L.R. 1075.

[331] See Karaliota v. Republic (1985) 3 C.L.R. 2053.

[332] Judgment delivered by Gavrielides J.

(Article 53.4). It is judicially settled that such action is not subject to judicial review (see inter alia *Demetriou v. Republic 3 R.S.C.C. 121*[333] and *Ioannou v. The Police (No. 1) (1997) 2 C.L.R. 147 (FB)*[334]). Likewise, decisions of the Attorney General to initiate a prosecution or discontinue criminal proceedings are not subject to judicial review. Decisions of the Attorney General in this respect are referable, as judicially acknowledged, to the judicial domain of power. Control, if any, of such decisions can only be exercised by a competent court of law (see *Republic v. Zacharia 2 R.S.C.C. 1*[335] and *Xenofontos v. Republic 2 R.S.C.C. 89*[336]). Also complaints referable to the exercise of the power to prosecute crime are, for similar reasons, not justiciable under Article 146.1 (see *Pitsillos v. Attorney General (1998) 3 C.L.R. 266 (FB)*[337]). The victim of crime is not remediless; he/she can institute a private prosecution against the perpetrator, a right recognised by the common law as a fundamental freedom of the individual (see *Ttofinis v. Theocharides (1983) 2 C.L.R. 363 (CA)*[338]).

Decisions of the Supreme Council of Judicature (composed of the Judges of the Supreme Court) involving the appointment, transfer, promotion or discipline of Judges are not subject to judicial review notwithstanding their administrative insignias. They do not derive from the exercise of executive or administrative power. Such acts are interwoven with the exercise of judicial power. The justiciability of such decisions came up for review in *Antonis Kourris v. The Supreme Council of Judicature (1972) 3 C.L.R. 390 (FB)*,[339] a majority decision, where it was held that such decisions are not reviewable because they do not emanate from the exercise of administrative power. They are associated with the domain of the judicial power and the promotion of its ends. The same stand was adopted in a subsequent decision where a similar question was raised for consideration in *Karatsis v. The Supreme Council of Judicature (2001) 3 C.L.R. 220 (P)*.[340]

[333] Judgment of the Court read by Forsthoff P.

[334] Judgment delivered by Pikis P. and Nicolaou J.

[335] The judgment of the Court was read by Forsthoff P.

[336] The judgment of the Court was read by Forsthoff P.

[337] Judgment delivered by Pikis P.

[338] Judgment delivered by Pikis J.

[339] Majority judgment delivered by Triantafyllides P., minority judgments delivered by Hadjianastassiou J. and A Loizou J.

[340] Judgment delivered by Pikis P.

16 By the same token, regulations and by-laws issued by an organ of the Executive in exercise of legislative power delegated to them by law are not subject to judicial review. They qualify as legislation, be it of a subsidiary nature, beyond the realm of judicial review (see *Westpark Ltd. v. Republic (1987) 3 C.L.R. 1473 (SJ)*[341]).

Article 146.1 confines judicial review to the validity of an act, decision or omission deriving from the exercise of administrative or executive authority. Of course, a justiciable act or decision founded on legislation – disputed as unconstitutional – may be challenged by reference to the unconstitutionality of the law wherefrom it derives. Consequently, an act founded on an unconstitutional piece of legislation is tainted by unconstitutionality and must on that account be annulled.

17 The Administration may by the same act or decision often bearing the appearance of an order resolve matters affecting more than one persons. Such orders bear a degree of resemblance to regulations but they must not be confused with them. Orders of the Administration divisible into a multitude of individual administrative acts or decisions are amenable to judicial review in the same way that singular decisions may be impugned by the person affected thereby. The differences between regulatory acts issued by the Administration and acts determinative of the rights and obligations of persons under the law were explored in *Demetriades a.o. v. Council of Ministers a.o. (1996) 3 C.L.R. 85 (FB)*.[342] At issue was the character of zoning orders defining the uses to which land situated in different parts of the island could be put. Did the orders constitute a regulation or a multiple administrative act? This question was decided preliminary to any inquiry into the substance of the recourses in order to determine the justiciability of the subject matter of the proceedings. The Court upheld the proceedings as setting forth for review justiciable acts emanating from the exercise of executive authority after reminding that the substantive nature of the act – as opposed to the form in which it is presented or that envelopes it – provides the test for the characterisation or classification of an act or decision. The Court adverted to the nature of regulatory acts and acts stemming from the exercise of executive or administrative authority and pronounced:

> A legislative act is one establishing canons of law. An act entailing the exercise of executive authority is one determinative of the framework of governance

---

[341] Judgment delivered by Pikis J.
[342] Judgment delivered by Pikis P.

and the implementation of the law. An administrative act is one deriving from the application of the law to the particular circumstances of a case. The necessity for the imposition of zoning orders involves the exercise of executive power whereas the determination of their content involves the exercise of administrative authority.[343]

Policy decisions of the Administration, that is decisions defining or earmarking the approach of the Administration to the exercise of its powers, are not subject to judicial review. They are not productive in themselves of legal consequences for the subject but their application in the decision making process may be contested if legally objectionable. The justiciability of government policy as distinct from administrative decisions taken in furtherance thereto came up for consideration in *Aphroditi Ltd. v. Republic (1986) 3 C.L.R. 1555 (SJ)*.[344] What gave rise to the recourse was the refusal of the Minister of Commerce and Industry to change government policy with regard to the regime of protection of the production of matches afforded to local industry. The Minister declared, there was no justification for any change in the existing policy reflected in the relevant Regulations. Moving along the path charted by earlier authority,[345] the Court affirmed "in any event administrative policy as distinct from administrative action is not a proper subject for review by the Courts". The Court added: "For its policies as distinct from its actions, the executive is only politically accountable". *18*

## IV. Test of Legality of Acts, Decisions and Omissions of the Administration

A justiciable act, decision or omission will be invalidated if, as provided in Article 146.1, it "is contrary to any of the provisions of this Constitution or of any law or is made in excess or in abuse of powers vested in such organ or authority or person". The review is intended to scrutinize the legality of acts or omissions and not to evaluate their correctness from the point of view of the Judiciary. So long as the Administration acts within the parameters of *19*

[343] Translation from Greek.

[344] Judgment delivered by Pikis J.

[345] See inter alia Savvidou v. The Republic (1970) 3 C.L.R. 118; Pernaros v. The Republic (1975) 3 C.L.R. 175.

the law, in furtherance to its purposes and according to the norms of good administration, the public authority trusted with the power to determine a given matter is the arbiter of its decisions. Any choice between alternative courses rests entirely with it. The Judiciary does not intrude into the province of the Administration. The jurisdiction of the Court under Article 146.1 accords with the principle of separation of powers. The review is confined to ascertaining (testing) the legality of the action of the Administration, a pre-eminently judicial matter. The decision in *Christofi v. Republic (1992) 4 C.L.R. 939 (SJ)*[346] adverts to the distinction between the judicial and administrative spheres of authority. This division is subject to the following proviso, namely that the Court may annul an administrative decision if it concludes that it was one not reasonably open to the Administration to take it (see inter alia *Sarruhan v. Republic 2 R.S.C.C. 133*[347]). To justify intervention on this ground, the choice made must, in view of the material facts of the case, be such that no body or organ in the position of the decision makers could arrive at. The apparent deviation from the principle of separation of powers is more a matter of appearance rather than substance; inasmuch as acting in a manner contrary to reason and good sense betrays abuse of power, establishing a ground for the annulment of the act. The application of the principle is illustrated by the case of *Hadjisavva v. Republic (1982) 3 C.L.R. 76 (SJ)*,[348] where the Court was asked to void a decision of the Public Service Commission on the ground that the applicant was strikingly superior to the candidate selected and in consequence his choice was arbitrary. In its judgment, the Court defined striking superiority as follows: "Superiority must be of such a nature as to emerge on any view of the combined effect of the merits, qualifications and seniority of the parties competing for promotion; in other words, it must emerge as an unquestionable fact; so telling as to strike one at first sight." Striking superiority must in the case of candidates competing for appointment or promotion emerge from comparison of rival merits as manifest and objectively incontrovertible; as much was underlined in *Nicolaou v. P.S.C. (1990) 3 C.L.R. 4666 (SJ)*.[349]

The criteria relevant to the choice of the most suitable candidate are laid down in the Public Service Law L-33/67 replaced by L-1/90 (merit,

[346] Judgment delivered by Pikis J.
[347] The Judgment of the Court was read by Forsthoff P.
[348] Judgment delivered by Pikis J.
[349] Judgment delivered by Pikis J.

qualifications, seniority). Overlooking the striking superiority of a candidate and choosing another in his or her stead is tantamount to an act of favouritism resulting in the deprivation of the civil service of the best available personnel. At the same time, it breaches the right of the complainant to equality of treatment by the Administration guaranteed by Article 28.1.

1. Constitutionality

The Administration is duty bound to act in accordance with the Constitution more so its provisions guaranteeing human rights, the efficient application of which is the paramount duty of every public authority (see Article 35[350]). The case law of the Supreme Court on the subject emphasises that respect for human rights must be uppermost in the mind of the Administration. *20*

2. Equality

Equality before the Administration and treatment thereby is assured by Article 28 as a fundamental right of the individual. Persons in the same position must be likewise treated. A distinction in the treatment of persons must be justified by differences in their position objectively discernible. As judicially acknowledged, homogeneous subjects or objects of the law must be likewise treated and heterogeneous subjects or objects of the law must be differently treated (see *Sergidis v. Republic (1991) 1 C.L.R. 119 (FB)*[351]). Logic should guide in the identification of similarities and differences between objects and subjects of the law. The existence of similarities and dissimilarities between subjects or objects of the law is broadly and not microscopically viewed. The test has to do with the substance of the subjects of the law.[352] A pertinent question is whether a dissimilar treatment of subjects or objects of the law disproportionate to their dissimilarities violates the principle of equality. Cyprus' case law provides no direct answer to the *21*

[350] It reads: The legislative, executive and judicial authorities of the Republic shall be bound to secure, within the limits of their respective competence, the efficient application of the provisions of this Part.

[351] Judgment delivered by Pikis J; see also President of the Republic v. House of Representatives (No. 2) (1989) 3 C.L.R. 1931.

[352] See also Republic (Minister of Finance) v. Nishan Arakian a.o. (1972) 3 C.L.R. 294 and Apostolides a.o. v. Republic (1984) 3 C.L.R. 233.

question. I addressed this question in my book “Basic Aspects of Cyprus Law”[353]. My answer is that different treatment of subjects and objects of the law cannot be disproportionate to their dissimilarity. Only dissimilarities can provide ground for differentiation such as corresponds to them.

In *Case of Thlimmenos v. Greece Application No. 34369/97, 6th April 2000* the European Court of Human Rights decided that in the absence of an objective and reasonable justification failure to treat differently persons whose situations are significantly different does violate Article 14 of the European Convention on Human Rights.[354] This decision lends, be it indirectly, jurisprudential support to the view expressed above that equality is an all-embracive concept not to be marginalized in any circumstances.

22 The right to equality legitimizes a person to seek judicial review of administrative action in virtue of the interest to be likewise treated as any other individual in the same position. In the case of *Elia a.o. v. Republic (1999) 3 C.L.R. 884*[355] it was stressed[356] that the right to equality generates a legitimate interest to have recourse to the Court to test the legality of action seemingly violative of the person’s right to equality of treatment. Equality of opportunity, as the Court underlined, is at the root of the notion of equality. In the case of *Elia* (supra) a law providing for the permanent appointment of temporary public service personnel without going through the process of selection by the Public Service Commission, requiring the advertisement of the post so that every qualified person could apply for it, was declared unconstitutional for breach among other reasons of Article 28.

In *Republic v. Constantinou (2002) 3 C.L.R. 534 (FB) (majority decision)*[357] it was decided that the right to equality admits of no restrictions. A law providing that a quota of positions in the public service should be filled by qualified persons severely stricken by the Turkish invasion was declared unconstitutional on account of inequality of treatment and sequentially breach of Article 28. Merit is the principal criterion for the manning of the public service. Candidates competing for appointment could not be assessed

---

353 Athens 2003 – General Department of Law Pantion University – A. N. Sakkoula Publications (in Greek).

354 Cited in: Campbell a.o. v. South Northamptonshire District Council and another [2004] 3 All E.R. 387.

355 Judgment delivered by Pikis P.

356 Menelaou a.o. v. Republic a.o. (1996) 3 C.L.R. 370.

357 Majority judgment delivered by Pikis P., minority judgment delivered by Nicolaides J.

by any standard other than ability to perform the duties pertaining to the office. Differences in the background of the candidates provided no ground for differentiation amongst them. The yardstick for comparison is inflexibly confined to ability. Stricken persons did not constitute a separate category for purposes of appointment to the public service. Merit was the only ground that could justify differentiation between them. Stricken persons could be separately treated where their disadvantageous position justified distinctions in their treatment compared to non-stricken persons. Something that was done by a variety of measures including the Debtors Relief Act treating non-stricken debtors and stricken debtors differently in relation to the discharge of their debts.[358] One may conclude that any distinction made in the treatment of a subject of the law must be justified by reference to the purpose for which the power is granted to the decision-makers. In the case of the staffing of the public service the purpose for which the power is given is to select the most meritorious candidates. Only distinctions made with reference to the merits of candidates, as may be the case with regard to their qualifications, can be reconciled with the promotion of the purposes of the law.

In *Koullouros v. Koullourou a.o. (1989) 1 C.L.R. 50 (CA)*[359] the Court held that men and women have equal rights and similar responsibilities. That is the premise for the identification, as the Court held, of the rights and obligations of spouses in the entire field of marital relations including desertion. Article 28 introduces the Aristotelian concept of equality, as the Court indicated, making the substance of things the denominator of equality as opposed to their numerical capacity or strength.[360] Homogeneity is defined by reference to the nature of things or the objective status of persons in contrast to their form. The test of equality has to do with the substance and not the form of objects and subjects of the law.

Illegal treatment by the Administration does not create a basis for equality of *23*
treatment. The principle is equality under the law and not outside it. Repetition of an illegal precedent would only serve to perpetuate illegality (see

[358] See inter alia Aloupas v. National Bank of Greece (1983) 1 C.L.R. 55.

[359] Judgment delivered by Pikis J.

[360] See also Apostolides a.o. v. Republic (1982) 3 C.L.R. 929, Papadopoulou v. Republic (1984) 3 C.L.R. 332, Pavlou v. Returning Officer a.o. (1987) 1 C.L.R. 252, Savvides v. Republic (1989) 3B C.L.R. 127.

inter alia *Koniotis v. Republic (1967) 3 C.L.R. 376 (SJ)*[361] *and Karayiannis a.o. v. Educational Service Committee (1979) 3 C.L.R. 371 (SJ)*[362]).

3. Conformity to the Law – Excess of Power – Abuse of Power

*24* The Administration must act within the bounds of the law and in accordance with its dictates. Subject to the Constitution, authority claimed by the Administration must derive from the law. The Administration is the custodian of the power given it, duty bound to exercise it bona fide for the advancement of the purposes ordained by law. Action outside or beyond the powers conferred upon the Administration by law amounts to an act or decision taken in excess of power and as such liable to be annulled. Power is abused when used for purposes other than those for which it is given. In that case the decision is fraught with ulterior motives. Under Article 146.1 excess or abuse of power constitutes distinct grounds for the annulment of administrative acts or decisions.

4. Prerequisites for a Valid Decision of the Administration

*25* For judicial control to be feasible, the Administration must keep proper records of the proceedings leading to a decision and the decision itself. Such records must cover the entire field of action. Keeping a proper record of the administrative process is a principle of good administration.

Judicial review is the forum for the examination of executory administrative acts or decisions. In the absence of proper records, the inquiry into the administrative process becomes impossible, judicial review unachievable and the ends of administrative justice frustrated.

*Medcon Construction a.o. v. Republic (1968) 3 C.L.R. 535 (SJ)*[363] *and Gavrielides v. Electricity Authority (1989) 3 C.L.R. 585 (SJ)*[364] are two of many cases where it was adjudged that the inevitable outcome of failure to keep proper records is the annulment of the act or decision forming the subject matter of review. The Administration is duty bound to produce the file of the case before the Court inquiring into the validity of its act or decision and make it available beforehand for inspection by the applicant. In *Dome*

[361] Judgment delivered by Triantafyllides J.
[362] Judgment delivered by A. Loizou J.
[363] Judgment delivered by Triantafyllides J.
[364] Judgment delivered by Pikis J.

*Industries Ltd. v. Improvement Board of Ayia Napa (1989) 3 C.L.R. 741 (SJ)*[365] it was decided that failure on the part of the Administration to produce its records before the court leads inexorably to the annulment of its act or decision.

The records kept must reflect adequately the legal and factual background to the decision. Furthermore, they must reveal the results of the inquiry into the facts relevant to decision making. Thirdly, the decision must indicate the reasons upon which it is founded.

The reasoning of a decision is all important for testing the legality of administrative action. A decision lacking due reasoning cannot stand scrutiny and will be annulled as a matter of course (see inter alia *P.E.O. v. Republic (1965) 3 C.L.R. 27 (SJ)*[366], *Maratheftou a.o. v. Republic (1982) 3 C.L.R. 1088 (SJ)*[367]). Due reasoning requires disclosure of the material facts upon which the decision is founded such as would enable the Court to review the decision in order to bring judgment to bear on its legality. The absence of due reasoning is only excusable when the reasons for the decision emerge clearly and incontrovertibly from the material in the administrative file; when they are self-evident (see inter alia: *Frangou v. Republic (1998) 3 C.L.R. 270 (FB)*[368]).

Holding a due inquiry into the facts of the case is another prerequisite for a valid act or decision of the Administration. Elicitation of the material facts, defined by the requisites of the law and the circumstances of the case, is of the essence. *26*

Misconception of the law materially affecting a decision taken exposes it to annulment (see inter alia *Soteriou v. Republic (1966) 3 C.L.R. 83 (SJ)*[369]). Misconception of facts materially affecting the decision made will likewise result in its voidance (see inter alia *Papantoniou a.o. v. Public Service Commission (1983) 3 C.L.R. 64 (SJ)*[370]). The assessment of the facts lies with the Administration and so long as the evaluation made and conclusions drawn therefrom are reasonably open to it, the Court will not interfere with a choice resting thereupon. *27*

---

365 Judgment delivered by Pikis J.
366 Judgment delivered by Triantafyllides J.
367 Judgment delivered by Pikis J.
368 Judgment delivered by Kallis J.
369 Judgment delivered by Triantafyllides J.
370 Judgment delivered by Pikis J.

Article 146.1 defines in plain terms the subject matter of judicial review; a complaint that the act, decision or omission was taken or allowed to happen in the latter case a) contrary to the Constitution or b) a law, or c) in excess or abuse of powers. To determine the validity of the complaint, the Court must inquire into the administrative process leading to the decision and the reasons supporting it. The object of the inquiry is to examine the legality of the action of the Administration in order to ensure that the decision was taken according to law.

*28* The complaint defines in broad terms the subject matter of the inquiry. No evidential burden in the form such burden takes in the adversarial system of justice lies on the complainant or pursuer or any other interested party taking part in the litigation. It is the responsibility of the Court to inquire into the legality of the act, decision or omission complained of. The burden of proof lying on the applicant, linked to the presumption of legality of an administrative act or decision, is a weak one going no further than requiring the pursuer to specify the reasons for which the legality of the act, decision or omission is challenged or contested. Of course, if the facts casting doubt on the legality of the decision are extra-administrative as in the case of allegations of bias of members of the decision making body, it is for the applicant to substantiate them to the extent of casting doubt on the impartiality of the body. The process of judicial review has an inquisitorial character. The inquiry extends, as often reiterated,[371] into every aspect of the decision, the background thereto and its reasoning.

*29* A party other than the complainant (named the applicant under the relevant Rules of Court) and the Administration (referred to as the respondent), having a personal interest in the outcome of the review, has a right to take part in the proceedings; a right acknowledged and its exercise institutionalized by the Rules of Court[372] regulating the exercise of jurisdiction under Article 146.1. Legitimation of third party intervention derives from the interest of such a person in the sustenance of the decision challenged; instantiated by the case of an appointee to a position in the public service,

[371] see inter alia Yiasemides a.o. v. Cyprus Organisation for the Dairy Industry (1989) 3 C.L.R. 2585.

[372] See in particular: Appeals (Revisional Jurisdiction) (Amendment) Rule of the Supreme Court 1995 (No. 5).

the legality of whose appointment is challenged under Article 146.1.[373] The intervener must have an interest in the decision taken akin, though not necessarily identical, to that of the applicant; arguably a more flexible test is applied in his/her case.[374] But the interest of the intervener in the decision must be separate and distinct from that of the general public.

The jurisdiction of the Court under Article 146 is delimited to the review of the legality of the act, decision or omission, not its correctness. Article 146.1 confines in terms the review of the impugned action or inaction of the Administration to the legal considerations outlined above. The correctness of the decision from the subjective viewpoint of the Court is not at issue except, as already explained, to the extent that the choice made defies reason. In *Christofi v. Republic (1992) 4 C.L.R. 939 (SJ)*[375] the Court reiterated that the object of judicial review is to ascertain whether the Administration 30

a) operated within the limits of the law, and
b) exercised its powers in accordance with the rules of good administration.

Judicial control is primarily directed to ascertaining whether the act or decision was taken within the proper legal framework (see *re Hadjisavva (1992) 1 C.L.R. 1134 (SJ)*[376]).

## IV. Article 146.2 – The Interest Necessary to Found Recourse to the Court

Only a person adversely affected by an executory act or decisions or an omission of the Administration prescribed in Article 146.1 is legitimized to seek judicial review of its legality. Article 146.2 restricts this right to persons prejudicially affected by the subject-matter of the act, decision or omission. This limitation may be regarded as an antinomy to the public law character of judicial review and the interest of the general public in sound administration. Roman law acknowledged actio popularis, that is recourse to the court 31

373 See inter alia Josephides v. The Republic 2 R.S.C.C. 72; Theocharides a.o. v. Ploussiou (1976) 3 C.L.R. 314; Vorkas a.o. v. Republic (1984) 3 C.L.R. 87.

374 See Yiolides – Charalambides a.o. v. The Municipality of Limasol (1988) 3 C.L.R. 972.

375 Judgment delivered by Pikis J.

376 Judgment delivered by Pikis J.

by a citizen activated by an interest in the proper application of the law. Such a remedy was first introduced in Athens by the Solonian legislation.[377] That actio popularis is unavailable in Cyprus was judicially acknowledged in the case of *Pitsillos v. C.B.C. (1982) 3 C.L.R. 208*.[378] The rigour of this exclusionary rule is – as in other countries that confine judicial review to prejudicially affected parties – mitigated by attaching a broad interpretation to the notion of "interest".

*32* Article 146.2 provides:

> Such a recourse may be made by a person whose any existing legitimate interest, which he has either as a person or by virtue of being a member of a Community, is adversely and directly affected by such decision or act or omission.

The prerequisites for the valid invocation of the revisional jurisdiction of the Supreme Court may be itemised as follows:

a) The pursuer must have an interest in the subject matter set down for judicial review, separate and distinct from the interest of the public or a section of it in the matter.
b) The interest must be directly as opposed to indirectly prejudiced, i.e. not as a reflection of prejudice to the interest of a third party.
c) The interest must be extant at the time the decision is taken by the Administration and must, as the case law establishes, subsist throughout the crucial stages of the proceedings, that is at the time the decision is taken, when recourse is made to the Court and at the time judgment is delivered.
d) The interest of the pursuer must be adversely affected presently, that is at the time the decision or act is taken or the omission occurs in contrast to future likely prejudice.

### 1. Existing Interest

*33* The interest must exist at the time the decision is taken. The likelihood of suffering prejudice in the future will not do unless prejudice to a definable interest is certain to occur at a future date (see inter alia *Hadjisavva v. Republic (1967) 3 C.L.R. 155 (SJ)*[379] and *Sergeant Georghiou a.o. v. Panayi*

---

[377] "Athenian Republic" by M.M. Sakkelariou (2000) page 22 (in Greek).
[378] Judgment delivered by Pikis J.
[379] Judgment delivered by Triantafyllides J.

*a.o. & Republic (1997) 3 C.L.R. 81 (FB)*[380]). As earlier indicated, interest must subsist at all three crucial stages of judicial review. Consequently, recalling the administrative act challenged by a recourse will sap it of its subject matter. To this, there is a qualification arising from the provisions of Article 146.6 that ties the recovery of damages caused by an illegal administrative act, decision or omission to its prior annulment by the Court. Therefore, if it does appear prima facie that damage was occasioned to the pursuer as a result of the recalled act, the proceedings will not abate. In that way, the right to compensation for injury suffered in consequence of an illegal act, decision or omission may be vindicated if the subject matter of the recourse is declared to be null and void. This is the state of the law as it emerges from the majority decision in the case of *Josephides v. Republic (1998) 3 C.L.R. 490 (FB)*.[381] The minority adopted the view that the ascertainment of damage cannot be examined outside the context of civil proceedings envisaged by Article 146.6. Judicial review is not the forum for such inquiry. Consequently, review of the recalled act should, in their view, be carried to conclusion if the applicant persists in his/her recourse.

2. Legitimate Interest

Interest is distinguishable from a right. As often said, legitimate interest is not equated to a right of action accruing upon breach or violation of a person's rights known to the law. Of course a person's rights, as stressed in *D. Ouzounian & M. Sultanian & Co. Ltd. v. Republic (1999) 3 C.L.R. 309 (FB)*[382], tend to define what may be of interest to the person. Because of this, the interest necessary to justify recourse to the court is characterised "legitimate", that is an interest originating or deriving from a person's rights. *34*

"Interest" denotes concern about something affecting a person in a tangible way distinguishable from the general interest of the public in the subject. The term "legitimate" that qualifies interest signifies the association of interest with the legal standing or status of a person. Interest may be either of a financial or a moral nature.[383] Financial interest is easy to identify, moral interest less so. In either case, the decision impugned must affect the

---

380 Judgment delivered by Pikis P.

381 Majority judgment delivered by Gavrielides J., minority judgment delivered by Pikis P.

382 Judgment delivered by Pikis P.

383 The term "moral interest" is used in the case law as a term of art having no association with morality as such. It signifies interest in an act, decision or omission arising out of a person's standing as a repository of rights and status.

pursuer in a peculiar or distinct way. It must affect persons in their pursuits as legal and social entities. The decision, act or omission must bear a nexus to the person of the pursuer. In *Sergeant Georghiou (supra)* a member of the police force was held to have a legitimate interest to challenge by way of recourse a decision involving the promotion of fellow policemen on grounds of heroism in the discharge of duty. Under the Police Regulations heroic conduct in the discharge of police duty merits promotion outside the prescribed course of advancement in the service. The Court held that colleagues of the rewarded policemen had an interest to challenge their promotion, notwithstanding the absence of any personal claim to promotion on similar grounds. Their interest derived, as the Court noted, from their status in the service and legitimate concern that rules of promotion affecting hierarchy in the police force should be duly observed. The inquiry into the promotions revealed that the acts founding them were nothing other than acts of faithful discharge of duty; not extraordinary acts qualifying as heroic conduct. On that account the decisions were voided and the police service purged of the consequences of misapplication of the law in an area of great importance to the police force.

3. Direct Interest

35 The prejudice legitimizing a person to have recourse to the Court occasioned by the impugned act, decision or omission must be direct. Perceived prejudice through the adverse effects of the act, decision or omission on another person will not do. Prejudice to corporate or unincorporated companies or associations does not legitimatise shareholders in the first case or members in the second to seek judicial review of decisions affecting a body in which they have an interest or an association to which they belong; their prejudice derives as a corollary of prejudice caused to another party. Only in the face of gross indifference on the part of the management of a company or an association to ventilate the grievance before the Court coupled with the imminence of the time for mounting a recourse running out may a shareholder or member of an association exceptionally be legitimised to mount a recourse; a sort of salvation exercise.[384] Conversely a company or association cannot take up as its cause prejudice to the interests of an individual shareholder or member. Airing their grievance is their business. A company may rightfully pursue a

[384] See inter alia Demetriou as chairman of CBC Staff Society v. The Republic 1 R.S.C.C. 99; The Bar Association of Nicosia etc. v. The Republic (1975) 3 C.L.R. 24; Cyprus Police Association a.o. v. The Republic (1974) 3 C.L.R. 152.

recourse for the review of a decision affecting its interests as such or those of its members in their entirety. The same can be said of the members of an association in relation to prejudice caused to the body. Undoubtedly, where prejudice to a corporate or an unincorporated body affects simultaneously and directly the interests of shareholders or members of the association, the latter can seek personally the review of the act, decision or omission in question.[385]

A decision exemplifying the principle, we are debating, is provided by the case of *Labourers Buses K. Petrou Ltd. v. Republic (1991) 4 C.L.R. 1929 (SJ)*.[386] Under the Administration of Estates Law CAP 189 the property of the deceased passes to his/her personal representatives, the administrator(s) or executor(s) of the estate. An heir, it was said, has no right to challenge an administrative decision affecting the estate; only the personal representative of the deceased who steps into his/her shoes can do so. The nature of the interest necessary to legitimise recourse to the Court for the review of an act, decision or omission of the Administration was examined in *Pitsillos v. C.B.C.* (supra). To begin, the Court stressed that provisions defining access to the Court must be construed broadly, as broadly as the language of Article 146.2 may permit. A similar approach is noticeable in Greece and France in interpreting analogous provisions of the law defining access to judicial review. *Actio popularis* is ruled out by the terms of Article 146.2. Judicial review may be sought by a person whose legitimate interest is directly affected by this decision. "Direct" in this context, as the Court noted, may be contrasted with "indirect" the antonym of direct. And the Court added "to be direct there must be an unbroken causative chain between the decision and the interest allegedly affected. There must be *legitimatio ad causum* in order to justify judicial review."

## V. Article 146.3 – The Time Limit for Challenging an Act, Decision or Omission of the Administration

The Constitution introduces a strict time limit within which acts or decisions of the Administration can be challenged by way of judicial review. *36*
Certainty in the sphere of public administration is a consequential factor for

[385] See inter alia Bank of Cyprus v. Republic (1985) 3 C.L.R. 636 and on appeal Bank of Cyprus (Holdings) v. Republic (1985) 3 C.L.R. 1883.

[386] Judgment delivered by Pikis J.

the efficacy of the process and fruitful planning. The wording of Article 146.3 regulates in mandatory terms the time within which a recourse may be taken by a prejudiced party after gaining knowledge of the act or decision.

Article 146.3 provides:

> Such recourse shall be made within seventy-five days of the date when the decision or act was published or, if not published and in the case of an omission, when it came to the knowledge of the person making the recourse.

*37* The Constitution does not postulate the publication of acts or decisions of the Executive as a necessary incident of their coming into being or their validity. Only laws or decisions of the Legislature must as a matter of constitutional order be published in the official gazette, the medium for the publication of laws.[387] Statutory law conferring power upon the Administration to issue an act or decision may envisage publication as a necessary step for their emergence. In that case, the publication is treated as an essential formality, a necessary incident for the genesis of the act or decision (see *Papaioannou v. Republic (1982) 3 C.L.R. 103 (SJ)*[388]).

Publication is a means of communicating an act or decision of the Administration. Publication in the official gazette, the official paper of the State, provides the medium of universal notification of a decision. For the notification of a decision, whether by notice in the gazette or through the post, to satisfy the requirements of Article 146.3 it must contain such information as to clearly inform of the decision taken and the prejudice occasioned to a person affected thereby who may in turn seek to vindicate his/her complaint against the act or decision through the process of judicial review. In the absence of such information, the publication will be ineffective as a means of communicating the decision and consequently, it will not set in motion the time for making a recourse. Indicative of the approach of the Court to this delicate subject is the case of *Pissas v. The Electricity Authority of Cyprus (No. 1) (1966) 3 C.L.R. 634 (SJ)*[389], where it was decided that a notice of acquisition in the official gazette providing inadequate information about the property to be acquired making it impossible for the owner to identify prejudice to his/her interest did not activate the 75 day period for recourse to the Court. The case law on the subject of notification of a decision to parties affected thereby signifies the strictness with which the duty cast on the

[387] See Articles 52 and 82.

[388] Judgment delivered by Pikis J.

[389] Judgment delivered by Triantafyllides J.

Administration to notify in this connection is viewed. In *Neophytou v. Republic (1964) C.L.R. 280 (SJ)*[390] the Court underlined that "... provisions such as para 3 of Article 146, which limit the right of access to the Court, should be strictly interpreted and applied and in case of doubt should be applied in favour of and not against the citizen ...". In the same spirit it was stressed in *Liveri v. Republic (1981) 3 C.L.R. 398 (SJ)*[391] that any doubt as to notification or the adequacy of the information conveyed about the decision taken will be resolved in favour of the subject. The principles relevant to notification and the information necessary to fix an affected party with knowledge were reviewed in *Papaioannou v. Republic* (supra). The following propositions were distilled:

a) Publication in the gazette when required by law sets in motion the time limit for making a recourse. If parties gain knowledge of the decision from any other source, prior to publication in the official gazette, time begins to run from that earlier date unless publication is an essential ingredient for the genesis of the act.
b) Notification whether through the gazette or by any other means need not extend to every detail of the decision. Notification is valid "... so long as it adequately acquaints the party affected thereby of the result and the reasoning behind it ...".

Article 146.3 does not connect publication as a source of knowledge to the duty to publish a decision. An act or decision may be published in the gazette in the absence of a duty to do so imposed by law. In that case, publication, although not an essential formality for the issuing of an act or decision, satisfies the requirement of providing notice of the decision to everybody concerned; thereafter time begins to run for the purpose of having recourse to the Court.

The Constitution does not prescribe publication in any particular form. In *38*
the absence of publication, time begins to run from the date a person prejudicially affected by the act or decision gains knowledge of it. Knowledge must be such as to acquaint the recipient of the substance of the decision apprising the person of prejudice to his/her interest, earmarking the process for its defence. The source of knowledge is immaterial so long as it is one that would ordinarily be credited as reliable (see *Ploussiou v. Central Bank of*

[390] Judgment delivered by Triantafyllides J.
[391] Judgment delivered by A Loizou J.

*Cyprus (1982) 3 C.L.R. 230 (SJ)*[392]). The burden is on the Administration to establish knowledge on the part of the person affected by its act or decision and, as earlier noticed, any doubt on the subject will be resolved in favour of the individual. The principles bearing on the acquisition of knowledge came up for consideration in *Georghiou v. Municipal Corporation Larnaca (No. 1) (1998) 3 C.L.R. 197 (FB) (majority judgment).*[393] The plenum was divided whether knowledge of a decision gained by the affected party in civil proceedings through its disclosure in the pleadings of the adversary, the Administration, was relevant or sufficient to set in motion the running of time. The majority rejected disclosure by the authorities of an executory act or decision in the pleadings of the State in civil proceedings as a proper source or as a valid process of communicating an administrative decision. The minority, on the other hand, considered such source of information to be reliable having regard to its provenance – as credible as any other reliable source. Dicta in the case of *Hadjimitsis (No. 2) v. District Officer of Paphos (1991) 3 C.L.R. 488 (FB)*[394] indicate that knowledge of a decision gained from the opposition to an application for judicial review constitutes a valid notification. Comparison of the reasoning of the two decisions reveals a dichotomy of judicial opinion on the subject.

*39* After due notification of an act or decision the activation of the 75 day period for seeking judicial review of either of them is not suspended for any reason other than a wholly exceptional one referred to hereafter. The ordinary qualifications of the civil law to the running of time for purposes of prescription such as minority or absence abroad have no application in the case of the period laid down by Article 146.3. The only ground upon which time for making a recourse is suspended is force majeure,[395] i.e. extraordinary circumstances, natural calamities or their equivalent in the affairs of man that make impossible the exercise of one's rights. The case law recognises that for as long as a person is prevented by force majeure from exercising the right to have recourse to the Court, the running of time under Article 146.3 is suspended. In *Marangou v. Republic (1997) 1 C.L.R. 1715 (FB)*[396] the Court re-emphasised[397] that, save for force majeure, the 75 day

[392] Judgment delivered by Pikis J.

[393] Majority judgment delivered by Nicolaides J, minority judgment delivered by Pikis P.

[394] Judgment delivered by Artemides J.

[395] A concept conveyed in English law by an Act of God.

[396] Judgment delivered by Pikis P.

[397] See inter alia Moran v. Republic 1 R.S.C.C. 10, Marcoullides v. Greek Communal Chamber 4 R.S.C.C. 10, Potamitis v. Water Board (1985) 1 C.L.R. 260.

period for filing a recourse will run its course. In face of such exceptional circumstances time is suspended for as long as they last but for no longer. Whether given circumstances amount to force majeure is a question of fact. As much was decided in *Yialousa Savings Bank Ltd. v. Republic (1977) 3 C.L.R. 75 (SJ)*,[398] where it was held that the Turkish invasion and sequential inability of persons trapped in an area occupied by Turkish troops to move about freely and exercise their rights constituted force majeure.[399]

Force majeure is a state of affairs arising from cataclysmic natural phenomena, known also as acts of God, or extraordinary social turmoil in pari materia to acts of God, making in either case impossible the exercise of one's rights. In those circumstances failure to initiate proceedings within the time envisaged by Article 146.3 cannot be attributed to inaction on the part of the pursuer but to impossibility. As pointed out in *Hadjimitsis* (supra), the Court will not suffer circumvention of the time limit for raising a recourse except in a case of force majeure.

A person accepting an act or decision of the Administration forfeits the right to challenge it unless the acceptance is accompanied by a reservation of the right to seek its judicial review. In *Katsounotou v. Republic (No. 1) (1990) 3 C.L.R. 1213 (SJ)*[400] it is explained that the effect of acceptance of a decision subject to reservation is to keep alive the right of the reserver to seek its judicial review within the time limit envisaged by Article 146.3. If no application for review is made within that time limit the reservation lapses and the decision is deemed to be unconditionally accepted. *40*

## VI. Article 146.4 – The Character of Decisions of the Court in the Exercise of its Revisional Jurisdiction

Article 146.4 provides: *41*

> Upon such a recourse the Court may, by its decision
>
> (a) confirm, either in whole or in part, such decision, act or omission;
> (b) declare, either in whole or in part, such decision or act to be null and void and of no effect whatsoever; or

---

398 Judgment delivered by Triantafyllides J.

399 See also Sermet Kemal v. Redundancy Fund, 11625, 23rd January 2004, not yet reported.

400 Judgment delivered by Pikis J.

(c) declare that such omission, either in whole or in part, ought not to have been made and that whatever has been omitted should have been performed."

It must be noticed that a different wording is used for the validation in contrast to the invalidation of the act or decision challenged. An act or decision found to be valid is confirmed reinforcing the presumption of legality attending the issuance of such an act or decision. In that case, the administrative seal remains intact. On the other hand, an act or decision found to be illegal is declared null and void, relegated to inexistence. The act or decision is legally abrogated.

A decision confirming an act or decision of the Administration operates in personam, rendering its subject matter res judicata between the pursuer and the Administration. A judgment of the Court annulling an act or decision of the Administration operates erga omnes; it has universal effect (see *Mavrommati a.o. v. Republic (1990) 3 C.L.R. 3943 (FB)*[401]). This was declared to be the case in *Kyriacou a.o. v. The Minister of the Interior (1988) 3 C.L.R. 643 (FB) (majority judgment)*[402] followed by many subsequent decisions.

In civil proceedings, judicial decisions are as a rule binding upon the parties and matters resolved thereby are treated as res judicata between them. Only decisions bearing on the personal status of a party, such as decisions affecting the birth, death and marital status, bind the world at large (see *Nicolaides v. Yerolemi (1984) 1 C.L.R. 742 (CA)*[403]).

42 The rule of res judicata does apply to decisions issued in the exercise of the revisional jurisdiction of the Court, too. The applicability of the doctrine of res iudicata in the domain of revisional jurisdiction came up for consideration in *Pieris v. Republic (1983) 3 C.L.R. 1054 (FB).*[404] The Court affirmed that similar and equally strong reasons warrant the application of the doctrine of res judicata in revisional as in civil proceedings. In addition to the grounds warranting the application of the doctrine to civil proceedings (certainly with regard to a person's rights, finality in litigation and sustenance of the efficacy of the judicial process), the doctrine of separation of powers necessitates its application in judicial review proceedings. The prerequisites for

[401] Judgment delivered by Pikis J.

[402] Majority judgment delivered by Pikis J; minority judgment delivered by Savvides J. It must be noted that the dissent affected a different issue raised in the proceedings respecting the procedural prerequisites for invoking the process of contempt of Court.

[403] Judgment delivered by Pikis J.

[404] Judgment delivered by Pikis J.

the application of res judicata are essentially the same in both areas of the law; importing a) adjudication on the merits, b) resolution of the point at issue by the judgment of the Court, directly or by necessary implication.

A decision voided by the Court must be re-examined by the Administration by reference to the factual background obtaining at the time the decision was taken. In the re-examination that follows, the decision makers must take stock of the judgment of the Court and give effect to it. Thus, in *Tornaris v. Republic (1983) 3 C.L.R. 1292 (SJ)*[405] the Court annulled a decision taken in disregard of the operative findings of the Court made upon review of the first attempt to fill the post to the effect that the applicant was strikingly superior to the selected candidate. In virtue of the provisions of Article 146.5 a decision of the Court given under Article 146.4 is binding "... on the Courts and all organs or authorities of the Republic ...". Likewise, in *Raftopoulos v. Republic, 513/93, 19 January 1998*, the Court annulled a decision of the Administration founded on facts contradicting an operative finding of the Court on the same subject made in an earlier decision. Consequently, res iudicata in the field of revisional jurisdiction raises an estoppel to the relitigation of issues resolved in the prior proceedings and binds the administrative organ on re-examination to give effect to what had been decided. Not only the operative findings of a court of revisional jurisdiction but findings on side or peripheral issues must not go unnoticed either. As explained in *Constantiou v. CYTA (1972) 3 C.L.R. 116 (SJ)*[406] and subsequently in *Gava v. Republic (1984) 3 C.L.R. 1391 (SJ)*,[407] such peripheral findings must be duly heeded requiring the supply of reasons of any departure therefrom upon re-examination. *43*

In the case of omissions, the form of the judgment is again declaratory. It declares the omission to discharge a duty as one that ought not to have happened and orders the doing of what ought to have been done. One may consider such a directive as an anomaly in a system of separation of powers in that the Administration is ordered to do something. However, the order is restricted to the discharge of a legal duty that the Administration has no discretion to refuse to carry out. The discharge of a legal duty by the Administration or a person for that matter is an obligation for the non-carrying out of which there can be no excuse. Thus, the declaration of the Court is nothing other

[405] Judgment delivered by Pikis J.

[406] Judgment delivered by A Loizou J.

[407] Judgment delivered by Pikis J.

than an order to carry out a duty imposed by law, a matter within the province of the judicial power.

44 An act may be confirmed or annulled in whole or in part as specified in (a) and (b) of paragraph 4 of Article 146, respectively. For this to be possible, the decision under review must be amenable to segregation or severance. Partial confirmation or voidance is easy when the decision under review is composite. If not, it must be multifaceted, amenable to division into its component parts. The Court will not reconstruct a decision of the Administration through the purging of its illegal parts.

## VII. Article 146.5 – Binding Character of Decisions

45 Decisions of the Court under Article 146.4 are binding upon all organs and authorities of the Republic. A duty is cast upon the organ or authority that issued the annulled act or decision to eradicate it and remove its effects with a view to restoring the status quo ante. Article 146.5 provides:

> Any decision given under paragraph 4 of this Article shall be binding on all courts and all organs or authorities in the Republic and shall be given effect to and acted upon by the organ or authority or person concerned.

A decision under paragraph 4 of Article 146 must be heeded and be given effect to by every power of the State; nothing inconsistent with or contradictory to this duty should be allowed or suffered. Moreover, a positive duty is cast upon the organ or authority that issued a voided act or decision to erase it and remove its after-effects cleansing the Administration of the illegal act. Such was declared in *Nissiotou v. Republic (1983) 3 C.L.R. 1483 (SJ)*[408] to be the effect of Article 146.5 exposing parties to the proceedings and third parties disobeying the judgment to punishment for contempt of court, a sanction provided for in Article 150 which reads:

> The Supreme Constitutional Court shall have jurisdiction to punish for contempt of itself.

The Court rejected the view that the only remedy available to an aggrieved person is the right to have recourse to the Court anew for a declaration that the non-compliance must be remedied as acknowledged by earlier authority.

---

[408] Judgment delivered by Pikis J.

The decision in *Nissiotou* (supra) on the point was approved on appeal in *Republic v. Nissiotou (1985) 3 C.L.R. 1335 (FB)*[409], the following passage from which is indicative of the approach to the subject:

> In our opinion only paragraph 4 of Article 146 of the Constitution provides about the remedies to be granted in recourse under such Article; and paragraph 5 of Article 145 does not provide for a separate remedy but can only be invoked in relation to an application for contempt of court under Article 150 of the Constitution.

The above decision was followed in *Kyriacou v. Minister of the Interior* (supra). The following passage from the judgment of the Court defines its position on the subject:

> Therefore, as a matter of principle, analysis of the provisions of paras. 4 and 5 of Art. 146 of the Constitution and authority, para. 5 of Art. 146 imposes a duty of active compliance, as earlier indicated, for breach of which a person may be committed for contempt under Art. 150 of the Constitution.[410]

The minority confined itself to the applicability of the relevant provisions of the Civil Procedure Rules for the invocation of the process of contempt holding them, contrary to the majority, applicable in all contempt proceedings. This being their stand, it sealed for them the outcome of the appeal, as the aforesaid rules were not applied. Hence, they did not address amenity to indict a person for contempt in face of non-compliance with a judgment of the Court.

The applicability of the process of contempt of court for disobedience of judgments given under paragraph 4 of Article 146 came up before the Supreme Court repeatedly. Power to punish for disobedience of orders of the court may be deemed to inhere in a court of law. Such jurisdiction does without doubt vest in courts exercising civil and criminal jurisdiction. Article 162 acknowledges such jurisdiction to civil and criminal courts, specifying that such a power includes the use of imprisonment as a means of coercing a person to comply with a judgment or order of the court; provided the length of it does not exceed twelve months. Article 150 confers similar jurisdiction on the Supreme Constitutional Court but without any limitation as to the period of imprisonment that may be imposed. Amenity on the part of the Supreme Court to invoke Article 150 in aid of enforcement of *46*

[409] Judgment delivered by Triantafyllides P.

[410] Judgment by Pikis J. at page 648.

its judgments came up for consideration in the case of *Vyronas v. Republic (1999) 3 C.L.R. 77 (FB) (majority decision).*[411] The Court was confronted with earlier conflicting decisions respecting the jurisdiction of the Supreme Court to punish persons disobeying judgments of the Court issued in the exercise of revisional jurisdiction for contempt. In the decision immediately before *Vyronas* (supra), namely *Republic v. Thalassinou (1991) 3 C.L.R. 203 (FB) (majority decision),*[412] the Court departed from earlier authority[413] that persons disobeying judgments given under Article 146.4 are liable to be punished for contempt of court. In *Vyronas* (supra) the majority accepted the last decision as definitive of the legal position on the issue. The principal reason for which the Supreme Court in *Vyronas* (supra) departed from earlier authority stemmed from the absence of provision in Article 150 for the punishment that may be imposed for contempt, invoking in this connection Article 12.1 that lays down that there should be no punishment in the absence of legal provision criminalising conduct. Moreover, they felt bound to follow the decision in *Thalassinou* (supra) as a matter of judicial precedent. They judged that the issue had been definitively settled in the above case by reference to the principles governing stare decisis. The minority too concerned itself with binding precedent. Majority and minority referred extensively to the decision of *Mavrogenis v. House of Representatives a.o. (No. 3) (1996) 1 C.L.R. 315 (P) (majority judgment)*[414] on the subject. The minority felt free, in the light of the principles governing precedent,[415] to choose between earlier conflicting authority; a freedom acknowledged in a number of earlier cases. In their view Article 150 incorporates what in reality is an inherent power of the court, no different from that conferred by Article 162 to a civil court, a power necessary in either case for the efficacy of the judicial process. The inherent powers of the court are indispensable for the effectiveness of the judicial process.[416] In the absence of power to oversee and ensure

---

[411] Majority decisions delivered by Nicolaides J, Nicolaou J. and Artemides J, minority decision delivered by Pikis P.

[412] Majority judgment delivered by A. Loizou P., minority judgments by Nikitas J. and Artemides J.

[413] Ioannides v. The Republic a.o. (1971) 3 C.L.R. 8 (FB), Republic v. Nissiotou (1985) 3 C.L.R. 1335 and Kyriacou v. Minister of Interior (1988) 3 C.L.R. 643.

[414] Majority judgment delivered by Pikis P.; minority judgment delivered by Artemides J. and Nicolaou J.

[415] Caspi Shipping Ltd. a.o. v. The Product of the Sales of Ship "Saphire Seas" (1998) 1 C.L.R. 1015 and Josephides v. Republic (1998) 3 C.L.R. 490.

[416] Charalambide v. Melodia (Charalambidou) (1997) 1 C.L.R. 724.

the execution of judicial decisions, the authority of the Court is muted and its autonomy undermined to the detriment of the rule of law. The minority pointed out that it cannot be disputed that disobedience to a decision of the Court is an act of contempt of court. What Article 150 establishes in their view, is to acknowledge jurisdiction to the Court to punish for contempt. It is a specific constitutional provision intended to strengthen the armoury of the law in the interest of law enforcement. Punishment in the case of contempt is not an end in itself but a means to an end, a coercive measure designed to ensure obedience to the judgment or order of the Court (see *Xenofontos v. Electricity Authority of Cyprus (2002) 3 C.L.R. 123 (FB)*[417]).

Upon the annulment of an act or decision of the Administration, the person, organ or authority that issued it comes under a duty to re-examine the subject of the voided decision. Re-examination of the subject for decision must be held within the context of the legal and factual background that obtained at the time the decision was taken or the act issued. In case of a change in the composition of the body that took the decision, findings resting on a subjective evaluation of facts made by the organ or authority in its original composition such as the assessment of a candidate's ability and knowledge at an interview must be ignored (see *Republic v. Safirides (1985) 3 C.L.R. 163) (FB)*[418]). A question that has vexed the Court is whether a gap in the factual background to a decision occasioned by the discarding of a fact material for arriving at a decision can be filled or better still reconstructed. The particular question the Court had to answer related to amenity to seek afresh the recommendations of the head of the department – one of the factors listed under the Public Service Law as essential for decision-making for promotions – in substitution for the original views of the head of the department rejected as faulty. By majority, the Court answered the question in the affirmative holding that it is possible to obtain anew the views of the head of the department, whether it be the same person or his/her successor on condition that the recommendation is based on the facts existing at the time the first decision was taken (see *Lyonas a.o. v. Republic (1990) 3 C.L.R. 1490 (FB) (majority judgment)*[419]). The minority took the contrary view primarily because such substitution defies the principle of restoration of the status quo ante; any attempt on re-examination to fill gaps by the 47

[417] Judgment delivered by Pikis P.

[418] Judgments delivered by Loris J and Pikis J.

[419] Judgment delivered by Chysostomis J.; minority judgment delivered by Pikis J.

introduction of new material – inexistent at the time the decision was first taken – entails the introduction of new facts, which is impermissible.

## VIII. Article 146.6 – Damage Resulting from a Voided Act or Decision or a Disowned Omission

*48* Article 146.6 provides:

> Any person suffering damage as a consequence of a decision, act or omission declared to be void under paragraph 4 of this Article shall be entitled, if his/her claim is not met to his/her satisfaction by the organ, authority or person concerned, to seek compensation through the judicial process or another remedy and to recover just and equitable damages to be assessed by the Court or to be granted such other just and equitable remedy as such a Court is empowered to grant.

To found an action on the provisions of paragraph 6 of Article 146, the plaintiff must have suffered damage on account of the voided act or decision or the unlawful omission. The damage must be a sequel to the annulled act or decision or the allowance of the omission to happen. There must be a direct nexus between the two. Another condition for the accrual of a right of action is failure on the part of the authority or organ concerned to satisfy a claim to that end by the aggrieved party. The measure of damages is that imported by the concept of "just and equitable compensation" (see inter alia *Frangoulides v. Republic (1982) 1 C.L.R. 462 (CA)*[420]). It is a more flexible measure than the one applicable to compensate for tortious acts under English law though not materially different. In both cases, restitution is at the heart of the exercise. The subject is discussed in the case of *Yiallouros v. Nicolaou (2001) 1 C.L.R. 558 (FB)*[421] in the context of a claim for compensation for breach of human rights. The principal equitable remedies that a court of law may grant are in addition to damages injunctions (prohibitory or mandatory) and specific performance.

*49* The wording of paragraph 6 of Article 146 is elusive and none too easy to interpret; especially difficult is the expression "if his claim is not met to his satisfaction by the organ, authority or person concerned". One may legitimately ask what does "claim" relate to. Does it refer to a claim for the restoration of the status quo ante or does it refer to a claim for monetary or

[420] Judgment delivered by Pikis J.

[421] Majority reasoning delivered by Pikis P., concurring reasoning delivered by Artemides J.

other relief on account of damage suffered because of the voided illegal act, decision or omission? One may contend that the use of the word "satisfaction" signifies monetary or other relief. Restoration of the status quo ante is the duty of the authorities in all cases, a duty imposed by Article 146.5 to be discharged independently of any damage occasioned to the successful applicant by the act or decision annulled or the unlawful omission. This interpretation would best accord with the wording of paragraph 6 inasmuch as the "satisfaction" of the person affected as such is made a consideration for the pursuit of a claim for damages. An interpretation along the above lines is reinforced by the acknowledgement of jurisdiction to a civil court to grant, in addition to or in substitution of damages, other equitable relief such as injunctions or specific performance. Such remedies are consistent with the empowerment of the Court to order the Administration to comply with the decision of the Court voiding an act or decision by issuing an order to that effect or possibly by the issuance of a prohibitory injunction restraining the Administration from acting upon the annulled act.

Judicial decisions do not reflect or support the above approach. On the contrary, paragraph 6 has been viewed as primarily directed to the restoration of the status quo ante and incidentally thereto the compensation of the party injured by the illegal act, decision or omission.

To begin, Article 146.6 is distinguishable from Article 172 that provides: *50*

> The Republic shall be liable for any unjust (wrongful) act or omission causing damage committed in the exercise or purported exercise of the duties of officers or authorities of the Republic. A law shall regulate such liability.

In *Phedias Kyriakides v. Republic 1 R.S.C.C. 66*[422] and subsequently in *Eleni Vrahimi a.o. v The Republic 4 R.S.C.C. 121*[423] the Court drew attention to the different objects of the two Articles of the Constitution and the diverse purposes they are designed to serve. Article 172 defines the liability of the State in contract and tort; liability covered by the law of obligations under continental law. Colonial legislation codifying the principles of contractual and civil wrongs liability saved, by Article 188, defines the obligations of persons in contract and tort and sequentially their liability for breaches thereof. Article 172 abolished immunity of the State for wrongful acts of its servants enjoyed by the British Crown in colonial times (see *Georghiou v.*

[422] The judgment of the Court was read by Forsthoff P.
[423] The judgment of the Court was read by Forsthoff P.

*Attorney-General (1982) 1 C.L.R. 938*[424]). Liability of the State under Article 146.6 is of a different species, interwoven with the duty of the State to restore legality upon the annulment of an illegal administrative act, decision or omission. The voidance of an act or decision or the renunciation of an omission does not confer a right to damages per se as decided in *Attorney General v. Holy Archbishopric of Cyprus (1999) 1 CLR 342 (CA)*[425]. This principle is exemplified by the case of *Englezaki a.o. v. Attorney General (1992) 1 C.L.R. 697 (CA)*[426]. The facts relevant to the decision of the Court were the following: Applicants were candidates for admission to the University of Cyprus. They successfully contested by way of judicial review a decision rejecting their admission. Thereafter, the University authorities re-examined the case in the light of the judgment of the Court and came to a decision likewise nugatory for their admission. The second decision was not challenged. Notwithstanding the restoration of legality, the applicants instituted a civil action claiming damages for loss suffered by the first decision that was annulled. The Court rejected their claim holding that they suffered none. The Court drew attention to the fact that the claimants had no right to be admitted to the University but only a right to be duly considered under the law as candidates for admission. Thus, they had an interest to seek judicial review of the decision. The wrong done to them by the first decision was remedied by the elimination of the ill-founded decision and the re-examination of their candidature in accordance with the law. The illegal decision was righted leaving no residual damage. To sustain a civil action, damage must result, as the Court explained, from the voided act, decision or omission notwithstanding the restoration of legality. In conformity with earlier authority, the Court noted that if the Administration fails or omits to restore legality, the successful litigant has the right to have recourse to the Court anew[427] and upon voidance of non-compliance the applicant may recover damages, if any, occasioned by the voided act. The case of *Pantelis Petrides v. The Greek Communal Chamber a.o. 5 R.S.C.C. 48*[428] suggests that if the voided action deprived the applicant of compensation due to him

[424] Judgment delivered by Pikis J., see also Alexandrou v. Attorney-General (1983) 1 C.L.R. 41.

[425] Judgment delivered by Pikis P.

[426] Judgment delivered by Pikis J.

[427] See inter alia Frangoulides v. Republic (1982) 1 C.L.R. 462; Kampis v. The Republic (1984) 1 C.L.R. 3141; Central Bank v. Theodorides (1993) 1 C.L.R. 420; Mavronihis v. Industrial Training Authority (1985) 1 C.L.R. 612.

[428] The judgment of the Court was read by Forsthoff P.

under the law, upon failure of subsequent negotiations to reach an acceptable settlement (the applicant was the victim of riotous acts for which compensation was stipulated for by law), the claimant could justifiably raise an action for damages for the loss suffered.

The case law is not altogether clear as to when a right to compensation accrues. It is certain that a right to compensation arises whenever, despite the restoration of the status quo ante, there is a residue of damage. In that case, there is no doubt that the injured party has a valid cause of action for the recovery of damages or other equitable relief before a civil court (see inter alia *Frangoulides v. Republic (1982) 1 C.L.R. 462 (CA)*[429] and *Central Bank v. Theodorides (1993) 1 C.L.R. 420 (CA)*[430]). What remains in doubt is whether a right to compensation accrues, provided always that damage is sustained, upon failure of the Administration to restore, following the annulment of an act or decision or the non-remedying of an omission, the status quo ante. The case of *Costas Tsakistos v. The Attorney General and The Republic etc. (1969) 1 C.L.R. 355 (CA)*[431] tends to indicate that an affirmative answer must be given to the question raised. To determine whether a right to compensation accrues, the Court set the following questions as crucial to the answer thereto: *51*

a) Has the appropriate organ or authority of the Republic given effect to and acted upon the decision of the Supreme Court, and
b) If the answer is in the negative, then what is the amount of the just and equitable compensation payable in the circumstances?

The ambit and implications of Article 146.6 and the direction of the case law on its interpretation and application came up for review in *Nicolas v. Republic (2001) 3 C.L.R. 983 (FB) (majority judgment)*[432]. Recitation of the material facts of the case is helpful in identifying the ratio decidendi of the decision. Under the Aliens and Immigrations Regulations (1972), the Ministry of Labour and Social Security may license employers to engage foreign personnel if qualified candidates are unavailable locally for filling vacant positions. Pursuant to such powers, the Ministry authorized a Cypriot air-carrier to employ for a period of 6 months foreign airplane pilots. The applicant, a *52*

[429] Judgment delivered by Pikis J.
[430] Judgment delivered by Pikis J.
[431] Judgment delivered by Triantafyllides J.
[432] Majority judgment delivered by Kallis J.; Gavrielides J. and Artemides J (concurring judgments) – minority judgment delivered by Pikis P.

Cypriot pilot, sought review of the relevant decision in proceedings under Article 146. As a result, the decision was annulled upon the finding of the Court that the applicant was qualified for the job. Nothing was done thereafter. Meantime, foreign pilots had been employed for the 6 months period. In civil proceedings raised by the applicant for damages, the Supreme Court rejected his appeal against the first instance decision dismissing his action. The reasons of the majority may be summarized as follows:

a) Firstly, as the claimant had not sought judicial review of the alleged inaction of the Administration to restore the status quo ante no right to damages accrued. A right to damages arises only if there is residual damage after the purging of the illegal act.
b) Secondly, the claimant failed to substantiate his claim to damage flowing from the voided decision. The onus of proving such damage lies on the claimant.

The minority on the other hand upheld the claim as justified drawing a distinction between the consequences of a voided act depending on whether they involve a breach of a right or a claim to acquire a right. Damage they pointed out results from a breach of a right not breach of mere expectation to acquire a right. As in the case of *Englezaki* (supra) the claim of the parties wronged by the voided act rested on an expectation to acquire a right. If that expectation is frustrated by the voided act, the remedy will lie in the restoration of legality by a new recourse for judicial review to denounce the recalcitrance or unwillingness of the Administration to restore legality. But, if the voided act entails denial of a right, as in the case in hand, a right to damages accrues provided loss is suffered in consequence thereof. In the instance under consideration, the Court had voided the act upon finding that the applicant was a qualified pilot depriving the decision of the Administration of every semblance of validity. In the process, the minority drew attention to the fact that to justify recourse to judicial review what is needed is a legitimate interest in the decision whereas to justify an action for damages a right must have been breached or denied. Dichotomy of opinion between the minority and the majority extended to proof of damage. Unlike the majority, the minority inclined to the view that it is always for the Administration to put before the Court facts relevant to compliance with a voided decision, an obligation deriving from the provisions of paragraph 5 of Article 146.

The measure of damages under Article 146.6 is just and equitable compensation. A measure that allows the Court to ponder and evaluate every element, factor and consideration bearing on damages holding the scales even between the parties.

# Index

Reference is made to chapter and paragraph number